How to Create Positive Affirmations That Serve You Better

12 people share their life-changing experiences with the 30 Days of Affirmations Challenge

How to Create Positive Affirmations That Serve You Better

12 people share their life-changing experiences
with the 30 Days of Affirmations Challenge

FAADA LTD, 1st Floor, 85 Great Portland St. London W1W 7LT, UK

bliss@faada.co.uk

A CIP catalogue record for this book is available from the British Library.

ISBN 978-1915944252 (E-Book)
ISBN 978-1915944269 (Paperback)
ISBN 9781915944276 (Hardback)

Disclaimer

The information provided in this book is for informational purposes only and is not intended as medical or psychological advice. The content of this book should not be used as a substitute for professional medical or mental health advice, diagnosis, or treatment. Always consult with a qualified healthcare professional regarding any questions or concerns you may have regarding your physical or mental health.

This book's author, co-writers and publisher have made reasonable efforts to ensure that the information provided is accurate and up-to-date. However, they make no representations or warranties of any kind, expressed or implied, regarding the completeness, accuracy, reliability, suitability, or availability of the information contained within this book.

The author and publisher are not liable for any errors or omissions in the content or for any actions taken based on the information provided. They shall have no responsibility or liability for any loss, injury, or damage arising from the use of the information in this book.

If you are experiencing physical or mental health issues, it is essential to seek professional help. This book does not establish a doctor-patient or therapist-client relationship. The reader should consult a qualified healthcare professional before implementing any suggestions or recommendations in this book.

By reading this book, you acknowledge and agree to the above disclaimer and understand that the author, co-writers and publisher are not responsible for any consequences resulting from the use of the information provided.

Preface

Memories of my youth are a bitter-sweet mix of love, laughter, great Jamaican food, loud music and even louder bouts of domestic situations between my parents.

They were often sporadic and unpredictable but I soon came to recognise when a storm was brewing. The silence was deafening, the air thick and heavy. At times I couldn't wait to be old enough to leave home. That time came and when it landed it was special.

A number one record, movies, video games, travelling extensively and meeting some of the most interesting folks ever. Truly mind-blowing. It has been like hanging onto a rollercoaster, climbing and swerving through a mirror into a magical world of endless possibilities.

Looking back now and after years of reflection, I recognise that my parents did the best they could. The pressure of raising children, dealing with racism in 1980s London and modest earnings took its toll at times, but my parents kept going. My mother was especially tenacious.

I'll never forget experiencing a number one record in the charts then having to sleep on my mum's floor, heading back to the drawing board to have another spin at the wheel of life. It was so tough.

Those feelings of grief, loss, anger, and sadness from childhood came back around with vengeance. But why was I feeling that way now when the fighting had stopped? The reasons weren't the same. How do self-affirmation and reframing make a difference? How long would it take for those feelings to go away?

As time went on I attended mindfulness-related courses, seminars, did a bunch of reading, and martial arts and helped others that had similar questions. During the Covid-19 pandemic/lockdown years, mindfulness became a priority focus. It was necessary during a time of overwhelming confusion and uncertainty. I went from reading bedtime stories to adults to offering stress-relief calls and group affirmation-making sessions.

However, this book is not so much about me and more about twelve very special people sharing their experiences with my approach to stress management using self-affirmation and reframing techniques. We avoid complicated backstories or science and get straight to the results.

Please feel free to connect, enjoy their findings and let me know how it works for you.

Thank you for trusting me Catherine, Cat, Cookie Williams, Daniella V Robbins, KF Plante, Lina, Mandi L Beacham, Masia One, Mindy Kittay, Perin Mehmet, Shirley Ann Felder and Valerie Paul-Kerry.

Contents

'The thing is not the thing..'

Stress, Trauma and Subconscious Choices

This is a very simple, "let's get things done" kind of book. Practical and hands-on, but it's important to set the scene and give some context.
Before we get into the testimonials it's important to discuss stress, the modalities and mindset that influence my approach.

Stress refers to the body's natural response to any physical, mental, or emotional demand. It is a necessary reaction that helps us to cope with various situations. However, prolonged bouts of stress can have a negative impact on our well-being.
Cortisol is released during stressful times to give the body a boost but when levels are constantly high, this can lead to digestive ailments, anxiety, diabetes, hypertension, heart attacks and more.

There are different types of stress that individuals may experience:

1. Acute Stress: This is a short-term and immediate form of stress that occurs in response to a specific event or situation. For example, facing a deadline or giving a presentation.

2. Chronic Stress: Often the result of persistent challenges, such as financial issues, relationship difficulties or work-related pressures. Chronic stress can have a detrimental impact on physical and mental health if left unmanaged.

3. Episodic Acute Stress: Some may constantly find themselves overwhelmed by a variety of stressors. People with this type of stress may exhibit symptoms such as irritability, anxiety, and a tendency to worry excessively.

4. Traumatic Stress: Occurs in response to a deeply distressing or life-threatening event, such as experiencing or witnessing an assault, natural disaster or otherwise serious accident. Traumatic stress can have long-lasting effects on an individual's well-being and often requires specialised treatment and support.

Becoming aware is essential for managing stress effectively. Sometimes experiences as far back as childhood, or even in the womb can still have an impact on us in adult life.
Parents divorcing, car accidents, being over-critiqued by your friends or family, having to parent your parents, bad breakups or the death of a loved one.

Another consideration is Epigenetics. This is the study of gene expression influenced by environmental factors and provides solid insights into the relationship between stress, trauma, and our life choices.

Dr. Bruce Lipton and Dr. Joe Dispenza have contributed a great deal to this field by highlighting how stress and trauma can affect our epigenome and decision-making processes. Chronic stress can lead to impulsive decision-making, as it impairs the rational thinking part of our brain. Traumatic experiences can result in unhealthy emotion-led choices as we try to stay safe and prevent the pain of the past from returning. However, we have the power to reshape our responses and choices. Practices like meditation, visualisation, and positive affirmations can create new neural pathways and promote healthier decision-making.

Modalities, Mindset and Influences

There are a number of approaches but in my stress management sessions and the 30 Days of Affirmations Challenge, we focused on fusing the creation and use of **Affirmations** with **Progressive Muscle Relaxation** and **Emotional Freedom Techniques (EFT)** to support the process.

What Are Affirmations?

Affirmations are positive statements that can be used to reinforce empowering beliefs and promote self-improvement. They are a popular tool that aims to shift one's mindset and create a more positive and supportive internal dialogue.

I specifically encourage the creation of affirmations unique to one's situation to make them as believable as possible and more likely to be impactful.

Research by Claude Steele and others has established the concept of self-affirmation theory. It suggests that affirmations can help individuals maintain a positive self-image and protect their self-integrity. According to this theory, affirmations work by reinforcing one's values and beliefs, reducing self-threat, and improving overall well-being.

Studies utilising neuroimaging techniques have shown that positive self-affirmations can activate reward-related brain regions. For example, a study published in Social Cognitive and Affective Neuroscience (2016) found that self-affirmation activates the ventromedial prefrontal cortex, a region associated with positive valuation and self-related processing.

Affirmations can enhance self-efficacy, which is an individual's belief in their ability to succeed in specific tasks or situations. A study published in the Journal of Applied Sport Psychology (2015) found that positive self-affirmations improved self-efficacy and motivation among athletes, leading to better performance outcomes.

Research has also indicated that affirmations may have a positive impact on stress management. A study published in Health Psychology (2013) demonstrated that self-affirmation interventions can buffer the negative effects of stress and improve psychological well-being.

To make affirmations effective, it is important to keep the following principles in mind:

1. Use Present Tense: To create a sense of immediate reality and reinforce the belief that the desired outcome is already happening.
2. Be Positive and Specific: Focus on what you want to achieve or experience, rather than what you want to avoid or eliminate. Make it clear, so it resonates with your goals and intentions.
3. Repetition and Consistency: Repeat affirmations preferably multiple times a day. Before and after sleep, when triggered or just for fun. Repetition helps reinforce new thought patterns and beliefs, gradually 'squeezing out' or replacing old, limiting ones.
4. Believe and Visualise: Engage with affirmations wholeheartedly and cultivate a genuine belief in their power. Visualise the positive outcomes as you repeat affirmations, allowing your mind to create a vivid picture of your desired reality.

Remember, while affirmations can be a powerful mindfulness tool for stress-relief and personal growth, they should not replace professional medical or psychological advice. If you are dealing with severe emotional distress or mental health issues, it is important to seek guidance from qualified healthcare professionals.

6 Important Considerations

Before we even get to creating affirmations there are a few things to note.

1. Affirmations work best when you reframe emotional associations.
   For example, a need for external validation, imposter syndrome, (not feeling worthy or deserving), procrastination (putting things off), lacking focus and consistency, identity conflicts, comfort eating, guilt when recognising your worth, struggles with self-love, finding it hard to create and/or communicate boundaries or carrying a fear of missing out.

2. Honesty about secondary benefits.
   Holding onto behaviours, people and choices because you fear losing something of perceived value even though the pain is greater than the reward. For example, staying in a toxic marriage because you are worried about what the rest of the family will say about divorce.

3. Let go of habits that no longer serve you and create new ones.

4. Create an environment that supports your focus. Remove yourself from toxic people, places and practices.

5. Regularly do something that scares you in order to reinforce your confidence with stepping into new spaces that serve you better.

6. Get used to saying what you want out loud. Write it down and say it like you mean it.

Question:
How big is your why and how much pain does it cause?
The more it matters, the more you're likely to do something about it.

How to Create Your Own Affirmations

There are many approaches but try this and otherwise adopt what works for you.

1. Find a safe space where you can sit or lay down without being disturbed.
2. Slow and focus on your breathing.
3. Become aware of what you feel from the inside out without judgement.
4. Visualise the other side of your challenges and create a positive sentence as if you have it already using 'I am', 'I am committed to', 'I choose' or similar.
5. Keep it positive.
6. Speak with conviction and say it out loud.

   Examples:-

   - I attract abundance.
   - I am financially free.
   - I choose to be lovable.
   - I am committed to being the best version of myself.
7. Journal, write them down. What do you notice? Go deeper by documenting what you feel.
8. Be consistent.

The 30 Days of Affirmations Challenge (30DAC)

As you see, it doesn't need to be difficult. It should be simple so it's easy to repeat.

Can you commit to 30 days like the contributors to this book did? Give it go!

- Commit to 30 days of daily affirmations.
- Listen to mine and repeat once a day.
- Create your own and repeat once a day.
- Document them in your personal diary and share what you notice.
- Email your findings to me and otherwise reach out if you get stuck bliss@faada.co.uk

Emotional Freedom Techniques (EFT)

Emotional Freedom Techniques is a practice based on a fusion of the Eastern healing arts of acupressure, shiatsu and reflexology with the Western approach to Cognitive Behavioural Therapy. More recently, EFT owes much to the work of Dr George Goodheart, the founder of Applied Kinesiology, and Dr Roger Callahan the founder of Thought Field Therapy (TFT). In the early '90s one of Dr Callahan's former students, Gary Craig, simplified complicated elements of TFT and made the process much easier for all to follow.

Me and my wife became practitioners by attending a course in Brighton (UK), run by Karl Dawson. It was a rollercoaster of emotions but we came out the other side seeing the world so differently and have gone on to make a difference in the lives of so many people since by using it.

How does EFT work?

EFT works by gently tapping acupressure points and making honest statements about your feelings in the moment. This sends calming signals to the amygdala easing you out of the body's 'fight or flight' response into a more relaxed state, clearing away emotional debris in the process.

It can also assist with reframing emotional associations created by past traumatic experiences.

Progressive Muscle Relaxation (PMR)

I also love to use progressive muscle relaxation. This is an anxiety-reduction technique first introduced by American physician Edmund Jacobson in the 1930s.

The technique involves alternating the contraction of major muscle groups in order to release tension in the body.

Fascia is a connective tissue that surrounds muscles, bones, organs, and other structures. It plays a significant role in maintaining structural integrity, transmitting forces, and providing support to the body.

When muscles are under chronic tension or stress, the fascia surrounding them can become tight and restricted. This can lead to reduced flexibility, limited range of motion, and discomfort. Fascial restrictions can affect not only the muscles directly but also neighbouring tissues and structures.

Chronic muscle tension is often associated with stress, anxiety, or physical discomfort. Progressive muscle relaxation can help reduce muscle tension by promoting a release of accumulated stress.

The Power of Breathing

Breathing exercises are another simple way to activate the body's relaxation response, too. They can promote physiological and psychological calmness, and counteract the effects of stress.

Belly breathing or abdominal breathing, is a technique that involves slow, deep breaths using the diaphragm. Research shows that this technique can activate the parasympathetic nervous system, leading to relaxation and a decrease in stress responses.

A study published in the Journal of Physical Therapy Science (2019) found that box breathing reduced stress and improved autonomic nervous system balance.

Box breathing, or square breathing, is a technique that involves inhaling, holding the breath, exhaling, and holding the breath again in a structured pattern. I typically encourage a longer count when exhaling. This technique can help regulate breathing, increase oxygenation and lower your heart rate inducing a sense of calmness.

Gratitude

Gratitude meditations involve focusing on and cultivating feelings of appreciation towards specific people, events, or aspects of one's life. Research suggests that engaging in positive emotions, such as gratitude, can regulate stress responses and promote psychological well-being. A study published in the Journal of Personality and Social Psychology (2003) found that participants who engaged in gratitude exercises experienced more positive emotions and lower levels of stress compared to those who did not.

Neuroscientific studies have shown that gratitude practices can induce changes in brain activity and lead to improved emotional regulation.

Gratitude meditations generally shift the focus of attention towards the positive aspects of life, fostering a more optimistic and positive mindset. This shift in perspective can help counteract negative thoughts and reduce stress.

Toxic Positivity

Toxic positivity dismisses or invalidates genuine negative emotions, often by urging individuals to "just think positive" or "be happy." This invalidation can make people feel unheard, misunderstood, and ashamed of their true emotions.

A relentless focus on positivity can lead individuals to avoid acknowledging and addressing genuine challenges in their lives.

While positivity can be beneficial, an unbalanced and unrealistic focus on positive emotions can have detrimental effects on an individual's mental health. This is why underpinning the process we focused on **Awareness**, **Acceptance** and **Action**. Feeling all emotions 'good or bad' but staying there only for as long as necessary.

The following form the basis of the mindset around my approach:

Awareness

Self-awareness plays a crucial role in stress management as it allows individuals to recognise, understand and respond to their thoughts, emotions, and behaviours.

A study published in the Journal of Occupational and Organisational Psychology (2015) found that individuals with higher levels of self-awareness exhibited more adaptive coping strategies and reported lower levels of job stress.

Acceptance

This is a core component of psychological flexibility, which refers to the ability to adaptively respond to challenging situations and experiences. It involves acknowledging and accepting both positive and negative emotions, thoughts, and sensations without trying to avoid or control them.

With a non-judgmental and honest focus, identify what you perceive to be the cause of the challenges in your life. Especially your own contribution to what you notice.

Action

Taking action is a crucial aspect of effective stress management. By actively engaging in behaviours and strategies to address stressors, individuals can regain a sense of control, bring about a sense of achievement, and fulfilment, reduce stress levels and enhance their overall well-being.

Asking yourself to explore the 'other side of the pain', create real measurable goals and do something with consistency to shift to a new space around what emerges from the first two steps.

Being mindful and again non-judgemental, as you allow yourself to be honest about what you feel in and around you.

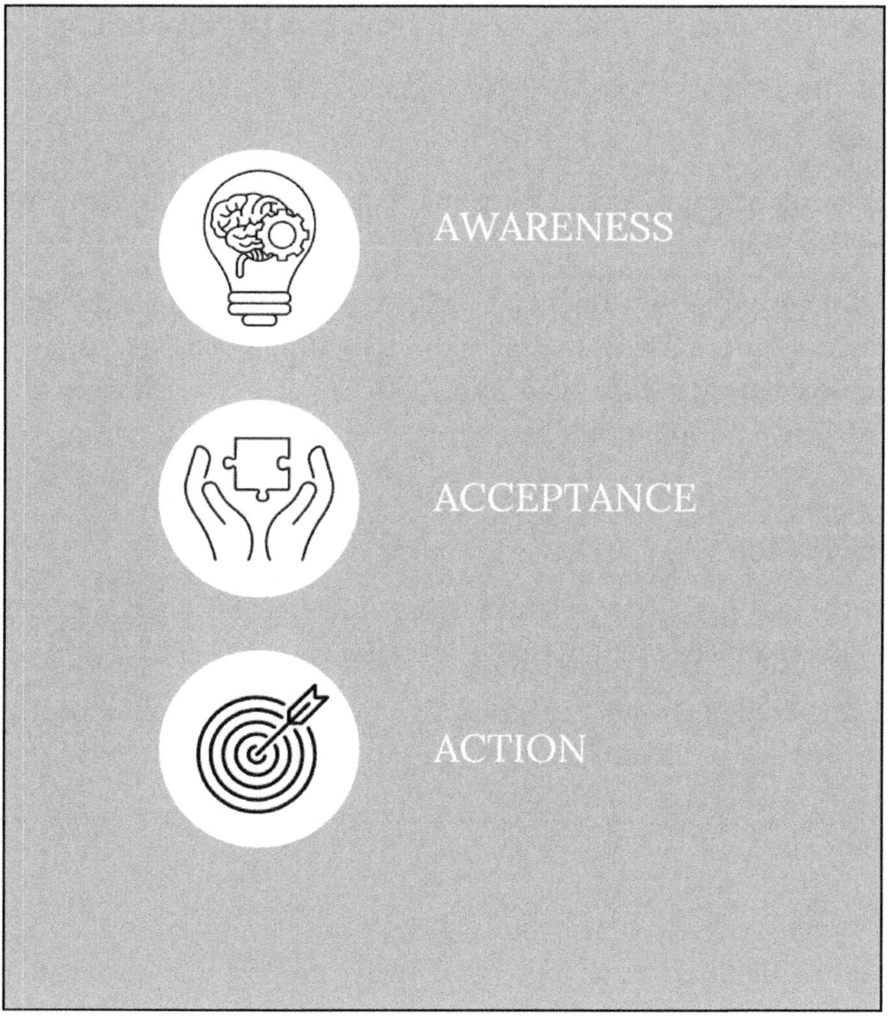

Freedom

Giving yourself permission to take a path of your choice guilt-free.

Letting go of the guilt associated with pursuing personal interests and prioritising self-care can have a significant impact on stress management.

This involves cultivating self-compassion, which is associated with improved psychological well-being and stress reduction.

Love

Creating a tangible set of actions that support and assert your love for yourself.

Self-love is closely related to self-compassion, which involves treating oneself with kindness, understanding, and acceptance. Self-compassion has been shown to reduce stress levels and enhance emotional well-being.

Ownership

With kindness, the identification of internal and external actions/choices that have contributed to your life challenges.

Acknowledging and recognising our role in contributing to challenging situations empowers us to make positive changes and develop effective coping strategies.

Worth

The recognition that you are worthy and the tangible list of reasons.

When individuals acknowledge their inherent value and develop a positive self-perception, they are more likely to adopt healthy coping strategies, maintain resilience, and effectively manage stress.

Journalling

Journaling provides an outlet for emotional release, allowing individuals to express and process their feelings.

It promotes cognitive processing, helping individuals reframe their perspectives and find meaning in challenging situations.

Goal Setting

Habits are formed through a process which involves the gradual development of automatic behaviours in response to repeated actions and cues.

- Cue: The first stage of habit formation involves a cue or trigger that prompts a specific behaviour. Cues can be external stimuli (such as a time of day, location, or visual cue) or internal cues (such as an emotional state or a particular thought).
- Routine: The routine refers to the behaviour itself—the action that is performed in response to the cue. This can be a physical action, a mental process, or a combination of both.
- Reward: The reward is the positive reinforcement that follows the behaviour. It is a consequence that satisfies a need or provides pleasure. Rewards can be intrinsic (e.g., a sense of accomplishment) or extrinsic (e.g., a treat or praise).
- Repetition: Repetition is key to habit formation. By consistently repeating the cue, routine and reward sequence, the behaviour becomes more automatic and ingrained over time.

- Automaticity: With sufficient repetition, the habit becomes automatic and requires less conscious effort and decision-making. It becomes a default response to the cue, often occurring almost unconsciously.

Goal setting serves as a roadmap for individuals to navigate through stressors and work towards achieving desired outcomes. Setting clear, realistic, and specific goals has been linked to increased motivation, improved self-efficacy, and enhanced psychological well-being (Locke & Latham, 2006). The process of goal setting helps individuals to clarify their priorities, break down complex tasks into manageable steps, and track their progress, providing a sense of control and accomplishment.

Traumatic experiences and stress can pose significant challenges to goal setting and habit formation. Trauma can disrupt cognitive processes, impair concentration and focus, and diminish self-confidence (Brewin et al., 2000). Individuals who have experienced trauma may find it difficult to set and achieve goals due to fear, hypervigilance, and intrusive thoughts associated with their traumatic experiences.

Awareness and honesty around resistance to change are important.

In such cases, it is essential to address the underlying trauma through therapeutic interventions like trauma-focused therapy, cognitive-behavioural therapy (CBT), or eye movement desensitisation and reprocessing (EMDR). These interventions can help individuals process their trauma, manage stress symptoms, and gradually rebuild the capacity to set and work towards goals.

7 POINTS OF MINDFULNESS

C.H.A.M.B.E.R.

ELROY 'SPOONFACE' POWELL

1 CREATIVITY

In 2015, psychologist and art therapist Dr. Cathy Malchiodi cited multiple studies confirming that being creative can increase positive emotions, reduce stress, anxiety, and even improve immune function.

What arts, crafts or creative activities do you enjoy?
What have you always wanted to try?

2 HEALTH & HEALING

'A UK-wide stress survey has found that almost three quarters of adults (74%) have at some point over the past year felt so stressed they felt overwhelmed or unable to cope.' - mentalhealth.org.uk

Trauma creates emotional associations and unless we address these emotions, they stay in our subconscious affecting our lives until we uncover, reframe and process them out.

What are you doing to heal from the trauma of your past?
What healthy habits could you maintain or adopt?

3 AWARENESS

In 2002, Anthony Grant, John Franklin and Peter Langford published their exploration of self-reflection. It is speculated that there are two different types. One involves people constructively reflecting on how best to achieve their goals. The other is where individuals attempt to understand, contain or dissipate their negative emotional, cognitive and behavioural responses.

How often do you simply stop to become aware of yourself from the inside out? What do you notice?

4 MOVEMENT

Studies show that there is approximately a 20% to 30% lower risk of heart disease, depression and dementia for adults participating in daily physical activity - mindcharity.co.uk

How do you incorporate movement into your daily routine with consistency? What do you enjoy doing?

5 BOUNDARIES

'Work-related stress depression and anxiety has increased in recent years' - hse.gov.uk

Establishing boundaries is a healthy practice. It keeps us safe and can lower our stress levels. When we're clear about our boundaries, people will understand our limits and know what we are and are not OK with. The people who don't respect our boundaries are the ones we may not want in our lives.

What's your process for creating healthy boundaries?

6 ENVIRONMENT

'Your genes are controlled by your environment, and more specifically your perception of the environment.' - Dr. Bruce Lipton

We create beliefs based on what we see and feel around us.
Our thoughts can have a direct impact on our wellbeing.

What impact is your environment having on your health and mindset?
What needs to stay and what needs to go?

7 REACH OUT

'It's easy to stop noticing the world around us. It's also easy to lose touch with the way our bodies are feeling and to end up living in our heads.' - Professor Mark Williams, Director of the Oxford Mindfulness Centre.

A brain imaging study by UCLA psychologists revealed that verbalizing our feelings makes our sadness, anger and pain less intense.

How often do you share what you're going through with a professional or someone you otherwise trust?
How can you be supportive to others without depleting?

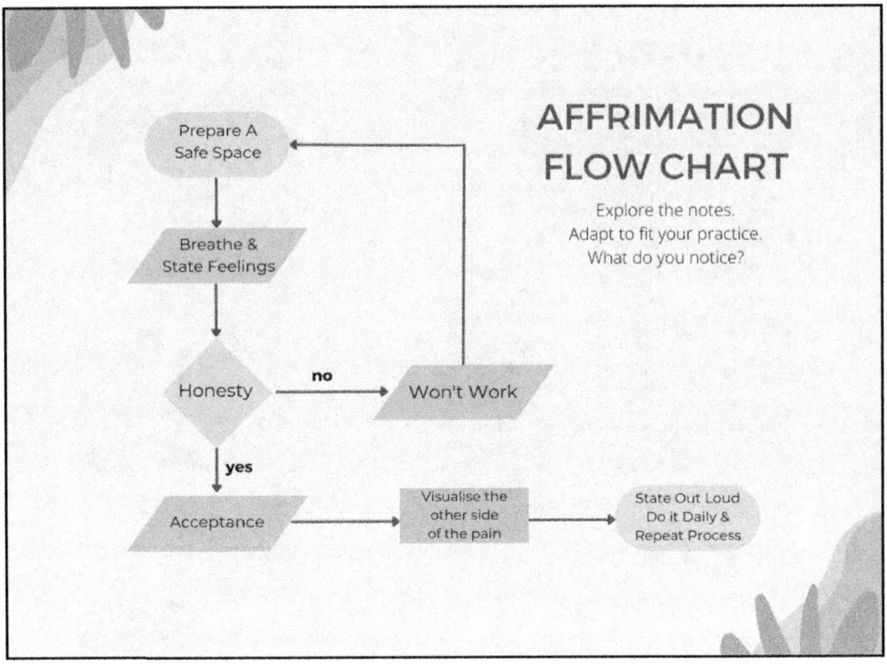
AFFRIMATION
FLOW CHART
Explore the notes.
Adapt to fit your practice.
What do you notice?
Prepare A
Safe Space
Breathe &
State Feelings
Honesty
no
Won't Work
yes
Acceptance
Visualise the
other side
of the pain
State Out Loud
Do it Daily &
Repeat Process

Testimonials & Affirmations

Everyone has a different approach when it comes to expressing themselves and sharing. It was important for me to make that a priority when sharing the testimonials here. Hence, you may see a different format and layout for each person's account. Enjoy.

Lina

Hi,

My name is Lina.

I want to start by expressing my gratitude to the Universe for sending Elroy my way a few years back. There was an instant connection and sense of clam and peace when I met him. Just the person I needed at that moment in time. For years I struggled with personal issues that stem from my childhood. Always trying to please others and putting myself last. Not setting boundaries, allowing people to take advantage of my generous and kind nature. Lacking in self-belief. Being made to believe I am not to achieve big things in life being a girl, because "someone" will provide for me.

When life didn't go to plan, I realised I needed to change all those restricted views that were embedded in me since childhood. Unlearn old habits and learn new beliefs. Practising mindfulness and affirmations with Elroy's guidance has helped me a lot with getting that process started. Joining the challenge for me was a way to keep the flow going, being able to grow through the experience with other wonderful people, each one of us on our individual journey, united by the same desire, to be better and stronger. I have been a Personal Trainer for over 10 years now and one of the biggest struggles for me has been growing my business. Not knowing how to progress,

Fearing being out of my comfort zone and a lack of support are all things that have held me back. Lack of self-confidence, family issues and not investing enough time in myself have contributed to all that. I finally feel I am making some progress with some of my business goals. I am challenging myself to work out things that I would not even have considered trying in the past. It is scary at times, but that is part of my growth and progress, facing my fears. Even if progress is slow, it is still moving forwards. I can recognise when sabotaging thoughts arise and can successfully replace them with positive thoughts.

I have learned to open up to the two most precious people in my life, my daughters. I had to put my pride aside and let them tell me where I was going wrong in our relationship. The love of a mother is unconditional but that is not enough for a good relationship with your children. They grow, so do their personalities. It was wrong of me to still handle them like little girls. Where we were all hurting before, we are now much happier and enjoy our company when we come together, knowing we are heard, and our boundaries are respected.

The biggest struggle during the challenge was setting a specific time for my affirmations. Although I would practice some before getting out of bed in the morning, my main affirmation of the day could come at any time. If I had to choose three things I enjoyed the most during the challenge, I would say they are:

1. The sense of inner fulfilment expressing gratitude brings

2. The change in energy affirmations provide

3. The manifestation of some affirmations.

Being grateful for the simplest things and becoming aware of them, made me realise how these simple things are of great importance in my life, the impact they have on me, how blessed I am and how much I sometimes take them for granted.

Acknowledging some thoughts are self-destructive, replacing them with constructive, powerful, positive affirmations, repeating them aloud, believing in them and visualising them, takes me from feeling low and bad about myself to knowing I can handle situations, even if difficult. Finally, attracting my affirmations and then seeing some manifesting themselves is mind-blowing! It makes you wonder where the limit might be and if there even is one. The biggest lesson I learned is I need no validation from others. It doesn't matter what others think of me or say of me. It is purely their vision and opinion, blemished by their emotions or feelings. I might be hurt but I will not allow

anyone to bring me down. I apply this principle with my clients when training progress takes a few knocks because of injuries or other causes. My motto is "we might bend but we will not break".

I feel I have learned so much about myself during the challenge, how strong I can be if I look after myself, when I channel the right thoughts into action, when I invest time and effort in myself, when I surround myself with the right people and cut out the wrong ones, when I focus on the positives instead of the negatives and when I look at possibilities instead of obstacles. Letting go of guilt for things I am not responsible for. Taking time for myself when life feels exhausting. Understanding I don't have to be pressured into decisions or actions, especially if I don't feel entirely comfortable with them.

It's ok to take time to reflect and let people wait. Those who can't wait are not worth my time in the first place because they do not value my feelings. Feeling good about being different if conforming hinders my growth. The truth is, I remember perfectly well what little curious little girl I was as a child. How I was always looking for new challenges and stimuli, things to explore and learn. Just because all this was knocked out of me by other people's beliefs of what my life should be like, it does not mean I have to keep doing that for the rest of my life. I can make the change, I am responsible for it and I will.

Once again, I want to express how grateful I am for this opportunity.

I started by saying my name is Lina and will end by saying I AM Lina.

Lina's 30 Days of Affirmations

1. I am committed to taking time for myself every day, to re-establish balance, serenity, and inner peace.
2. I am learning to communicate my boundaries with more ease and not feel guilty about them.
3. I am committed to having a productive day today.
4. No matter how stressful the situation, I will make time to breathe and think positively.
5. I accept the physical pain I am feeling and I will not allow it to stop me from living my life.
6. I am committed to living my best life.
7. I deserve to be loved and respected.
8. I am grateful for the comforts I already have and I am committed to making my life even more comfortable.
9. I am committed to success and create the life I desire.
10. I am, therefore, I can.
11. I am worthy of abundance. I am worthy of love. I am worthy of growth.
12. I deserve some me time and enjoy my own company.
13. I forgive myself for mistakes I made in the past and am committed to learning from them.
14. I love myself and free myself from external validation.
15. I attract my dreams and my financial independence.

16. I am grateful for the trust my clients have in me and I am worthy of making my dreams a reality.

17. I deserve a life free of pain.

18. I am committed to creating the life I desire. I deserve to be comfortable, loved, respected, happy, and financially independent.

19. I am committed to taking a breath and reflecting before I do, say or act upon anything.

20. I am grateful for the progress, however small, and attract more of it in all aspects of my life.

21. I am grateful for having less physical pain. I am grateful for the feeling of moving around more freely without the constant reminder of pain in my body.

22. I am committed to giving myself time and protect my inner peace.

23. I am committed to overcoming my fears.

24. I am grateful for the love of my family and friends and the support they provide.

25. I am grateful for the little things in life as they make a big difference to how I feel every day.

26. I attract opportunities that will allow me to grow my business.

27. I am on my journey to fulfil my dreams.

28. I am blessed, I am healthy, I am strong.

29. Even though I feel doubtful at times, I know I have everything I need to be successful.

30. I am working towards my goals and success with confidence.

Mindy Kittay

The first time I ever heard of, or experienced affirmations was at Agape Spiritual Center.

And the whole thing was life changing for me including that I felt like I had finally found home. The affirmations, which are a regular part of the service, really resonated with me and that they were making a difference for me. But I only did them on Sundays at the service. I didn't really think of making a habit of it or even creating my own.

Fast forward to 2020. The previous years had been challenging and had left me with some trauma and anxiety due to a loss of my career that I loved and 2020 came along just when I was starting to get my mojo back. I think it was a difficult time for most people. I felt lost, scared and depressed. I stopped taking care of myself and gained a lot of weight and was using crutches such as food, alcohol, on-line shopping and pot to just get through the days. I had no direction or idea of what my future was going to look like and that scared the hell out of me. I am a planner; I equate my value with productivity and making a difference in the world and I was stymied and lost.

Then I ran across Elroy "Spoonface" Powell's affirmations online, and I absolutely loved them. They were one of the few things that produced a state of calm for me and allowed me to really feel in my body that change was possible, that better things were ahead of me in my future. I reached out to thank him and to my surprise he responded personally, and I felt like I had made a real connection. Then he donated to my Facebook Birthday fundraiser! So, I kept an eye on what he was up to and kept listening to the affirmations and benefitting from them. His voice and the words are so soothing to me. I continue to listen almost daily. When he contacted me about the 30-day challenge I couldn't say YES fast enough!

All my life I have struggled with my weight and with negative self-talk. Instead of focusing on all the good things, the miracles and the manifestations, I would focus on the negative, the losses and the challenges. I have never truly believed that I am good enough, that I am not broken. I am always trying to improve and become more, not trusting that I am already enough. I have tried every diet known to man and I have a full library of self-help books. But nothing ever seemed to work.

When I decided to do the 30-day Challenge, my focus was on gratitude and trust.

Trusting myself, my decisions and my ability to take good care of myself and to have gratitude for all the beauty, joy, miracles and love that present themselves almost daily in my life. I am enough, my life, just being here is proof that I am enough. I don't need to be fixed. I am safe and everything is going to work out as it should.

I have taken several steps towards what I think of as self-healing. Even though I can still hear that voice in my head doubting and thinking that I am not enough, I am not good enough, strong enough, smart enough, beautiful enough, loveable enough, I find that the affirmations help to silence or at least calm that voice down. It enables me to STOP and take a breath and really look at all the amazing wonderful and brave things that I am doing. The daily affirmations really support this. They absolutely make a difference. I restarted my morning rituals of meditation, prayer, affirmations and journaling. I MAKE time for these, and I am chipping away at the "to do" items that I feel will help me the most.

I began seeing a therapist and for the first time (after many years of therapy on and off), I actually feel like I am opening up and releasing. I set aside a block of time to attend a retreat called "Freedom Embodied" which has been life changing. This was another moment of serendipity where a friend gifted me something that is exactly what I needed at exactly the right time, and I have begun to allow myself to feel, to grieve, to begin to accept myself and love myself.

Making sure I gave myself the time every day for my morning ritual, to do my affirmations and to create a special affirmation for the day was sometimes a struggle. When I felt like I was breaking through I would back off and schedule so much or in some way make sure that I didn't have the time. I had to face this lifelong pattern. I wasn't always successful. But every day I listened to Elroy's affirmations and could feel the tingling and the confidence build in my body. This was and is a joy for me. Having the opportunity to meet with him on Zoom and to work together to create some affirmations and build support for my journey was a highlight for sure. Creating my own affirmation each day, taking the time to really dive in and feel what was true for me was enlightening.

I always enjoyed saying affirmations and when I give them my full attention and really focus, I can physically feel them in my body. I believe that when we actually "feel" our emotions and intentions in our bodies that is half the battle. I trust that I can become the "real" me. I can be at peace which will enable me to give up my addictions and I am already living a life of more and more JOY every day. Working with Elroy and doing the affirmations has really started the ball rolling and I am excited and confident about continued success and happiness! I have so much gratitude for you Elroy 'Spoonface' Powell and I thank the Universe for putting you in my path!

Mindy's 30 Days of Affirmations

Day 1: I expel all past regrets and appreciate my courage to keep going forward. God loves me and I love me.

Day 2: Fear does not feed on the strength of my soul because I have certainty, confidence and assurance that all is working out in my best interest.

Day three: Today I am happy to just be me, as I am, because I know I am good enough. I trust my abilities to create and live the life I desire.

Day 4: I am centered and I do not let the things that other people do and say or external circumstances, rock my boat or upset me.

Day 5: I am willing and able to forgive the hurts of the past and move forward with love and gratitude.

Day 6: I have the confidence to face an uncertain future because I know deep in my soul that I will be fine and I am fine, no matter what.

Day 7: I trust in the future that everything will be OK and I do not waste time on worry and stress.

Day 8: I choose to let go of what I can't control and live stress free.

Day 9: I am confident in myself and my choices and I am able to speak my mind without anxiety and doubt.

Day 10: I remember and focus on all the beautiful, wonderful, positive things in my life and do not let negativity affect me.

Day 11: I trust my instincts and know that everything will turn out as it should.

Day 12: Only I control my attitude. I am excited and happy to be alive!

Day 13: I am excited about what the future holds and I know that the universe has my back.

Day 14: My heart is open to love, love is available to me.

Day 15: I believe in my ability to manifest my desires.

Day 16: I am a conduit for joy and happiness, both for myself and others.

Day 17: I trust my instincts and the universe. I am confident that all is as it should be.

Day 18: I believe in myself and my ability to feel joy, peace and happiness no matter the circumstances.

Day 19: I support my health and well-being by taking care of myself both physically, emotionally and mentally.

Day 20: I am ready and able to cope with the uncertainties of life and not let them rattle me.

Day 21: I am attracting success and companionship.

Day 22 I am surrendering to wholeness, peace, tranquillity and joy. Today is a gift and I am appreciating every moment of it.

Day 23: I focus on the things that I can control and let the others go. My time is too valuable to be fretting over things that I have no control over.

Day 24: I am love and I am perfect just the way I am.

Day 25: Even though I am sad, I am focusing on better times and remembering the joys of life. I am letting myself breathe and accepting that sadness is OK.

Day 26: I am grateful for all I have and all I am.

Day 27: I have the skills, the experience, and the knowledge to return my body to full health. I am taking care of myself by nourishing my physical, emotional and mental self.

Day 28: I am getting better at recognizing my limiting thoughts and turning those around.

Day 29: I am recognizing and moving past my negative thoughts and feeling confident about positive outcomes.

Date 30: I am blessed. My life is beautiful. I am grateful.

Perin Mehmet

Hey Elroy,

I just want to start off by saying thank you so much for including me on this challenge it has been an amazing experience and it has helped me in so many ways.

1000 Words.

On the day I was approached about joining the challenge I was at my all-time low. I was in tears every day; I could not see any way forward. I was in a rut. When the message came through asking me to join the challenge it was like some sort of sign to say get up and stop the tears. I accepted, the thought of starting something different was extremely out of my comfort zone, but with that being said it filled me with a sense of joy and I knew that I had to give this a go as I had to make a change in my life.

Before I started the challenge, my anxiety was at its all-time high, my mind was so trapped with all the past trauma, I would hide myself away, I would avoid going to any event, making excuses not to go to parties, avoid going shopping when I knew there would be a lot of people. I would constantly cry, forever feel down and low, started to lack complete confidence in myself to accomplish anything. I had not slept through the night for years. Every night I would wake up at 2am and be up until the early hours overplaying in my mind what had happened. I was angry that I allowed myself to become a victim of control and abuse. I felt like I had lost everything, I just could not see that I had everything I needed around me.

Now my life has really changed. I am sleeping through the night, I have attended some events and even helped out at my older son's year 6 leavers party. I go out more, I do not shy away from people and I feel much more empowered. The moment I knew the challenge had been working was when I had a hospital appointment to have an MRI Scan. When I arrived, I saw this machine and I could feel myself getting stressed. I lay down and they placed me in the machine, I had a panic attack. I asked to be removed and I had a total breakdown. I was crying I couldn't breathe but then I remembered the group and the affirmations that were being said. It gave me the strength to wipe the tears away and face my fears. I went back into the scanner and didn't move one bit and breathed just fine with not a moment of fear.

There are moments when past trauma creeps up on me and I get tearful, but I have my moment and I can pick myself up, whereas before this wasn't the case. I have also stopped comfort eating and lost almost 5 kilos in weight. But there is still a long way to go. I still have many hurdles in my life, but I am stronger now and I feel like I will be able to deal with the better without going into deep depression.

The hardest thing about keeping consistent is when you do have a down day or something reminds you of what has happened, then you find it difficult to stay focused and keep your mind positive.

The main things I enjoyed about the experience were hearing about other people's struggles and how they overcome their fears. It gives you a sense of well-being knowing you're not the only one. Having Elroy there was great. He kept you focused, checked on you to see if all was ok, and if you had sent any messages to the group. His enthusiasm and support were fantastic. His affirmations for the days encouraged you to keep on going. In addition, The group was filled with such wonderful people, which made the challenge very comfortable. No one judged and everyone supported one another. The group has given me so much faith in myself again and I couldn't be more grateful.

My number one takeaway is that simple changes to the way you approach your day make such a difference. Just thinking about what you want to make a change to or what you are grateful for, or even accepting even if things are not right in your life, that it's ok. You can approach it in a manner that will not make you overthink the situation.

If I went back in time, before the challenge I would not sit there and dwell on what has happened and what people have done to me. I would rise above that all and not allow people to have the control over me that they have done. I have allowed people to control my thoughts and feeling and even the way I should be. They took away my freedom, my confidence and my life was built around anxiety. I would never allow that to happen ever again.

Perin's 30 Days of Affirmations

1. I am doing my best.
2. I am grateful for my children, family and friends.
3. I will live each day as it comes and not stress about past traumas.
4. I enjoy the simple moments.
5. It is ok to ask for help when I need it.
6. I am committed to being the best I possibly can be for myself.
7. I am committed to staying strong and being able to accomplish everything I need to do today.
8. My feelings and needs are important.
9. I am strong enough to overcome difficult obstacles that are put in my way.
10. I have the strength to face the problems before me.
11. I can rise above the negativity around me.
12. I am getting better every day.
13. I am grateful for today and able to face my fears.
14. I am committed to improving myself.
15. I am grateful for this group as it has made me believe in myself again.
16. I am committed to moving forward and continue to make changes for the better.
17. I am grateful for the simple things in life.
18. I am committed to making a change.
19. I am grateful for the friends I have to support me.
20. I am becoming stronger every day.
21. I am grateful for all that I have.
22. I can let go of negativity.

23. I give myself permission to surround myself with those who love and support me.
24. I am grateful for my children.
25. I will face hard times with courage.
26. My needs matter.
27. I make time to take care of myself.
28. I am committed to moving forward in my life.
29. Today I will fill my mind with positive thoughts.
30. I am grateful for all I have in my life.

Mandi L Beacham

My 30-day Affirmation Challenge was a transformative experience. I wish I had incorporated affirmations into my daily ritual sooner because I have seen remarkable benefits over the past 30 days. I feel more relaxed, less anxious, and less likely to get uptight in certain situations. Additionally, I have learned to prioritise myself.

One of the main reasons I took on the 30 Days of Affirmations Challenge was to focus on self-care. My life tends to be hectic and chaotic as I try to please everyone, often neglecting myself in the process. I have realised that I need to make myself a priority. I also have a tendency to procrastinate on challenging or uninteresting tasks, struggling to prioritise them. This leads to feelings of guilt. The challenge aimed to help relieve this guilt and ensure I give myself some precious "me" time.

One of the most significant insights I gained was the power of reframing. I learned how to reframe challenging situations, negative comments, and general negativity. Through reframing, I became less reactive, frustrated, and angry in the face of adversity. Instead, I became more reflective, focusing on the positive aspects and putting everything into context. Repeating my affirmations during these moments made me feel calm, valued, and relaxed.

After completing the challenge, I made it a point to take time out for myself without feeling guilty. The relaxation aspect of the affirmation process feels crucial, as it helps me become more in tune with my body. Deep breaths during the process clear my mind, ease anxiety, and allow me to listen to my body, understand my feelings, and completely relax. It helps me focus on my affirmations. Throughout the month, I enjoyed vocalising my affirmations, speaking them loudly, and repeating them because I genuinely believed they were helping me. The entire process felt cathartic and cleansing.

The most challenging part of the process was initially starting the affirmations and finding time to do them every day. I realised the importance of consistency and making time to ensure I did my affirmations daily. Starting my day with a positive focus by doing the affirmations early in the morning yielded the best results. It made me feel purposeful, motivated and brought my affirmations to life. Some of my best experiences doing affirmations were lying in my garden, fully relaxed, listening to the birds, feeling the sun on my face and immersing myself in the beauty around me while letting the affirmations flow.

Occasionally, the affirmations didn't flow easily, but sometimes a simple one-liner like "I am enough" was perfect and all I needed. I realised that affirmations don't have to be complicated; keeping them simple, relevant, and pertinent to me was the key.

I thoroughly enjoyed the sense of community and family created within the group during the challenge. It felt safe, secure, and supportive, especially during challenging days. It was a joy to wake up and read everyone's affirmations, knowing we were all in this together. The "Affirm-a-family" was truly inspiring!

I deeply appreciate Elroy's support as he encouraged and guided us throughout the challenge with his knowledge and prompts. It made the whole experience fun, informative, and enjoyable. Reading Elroy's affirmations was also uplifting; we were all united in this challenge.

Journaling was another aspect I enjoyed. Writing down my feelings, affirmations for the day, and my body's response helped me reflect on my emotional state. Looking back, I can see that my anxiety has improved, my stomach is no longer knotted, and I feel motivated and relaxed. It confirms that I have experienced positive changes.

Engaging in affirmations is not always easy. Elroy reassured us at the beginning of the 30 days that the first 5-7 days might bring up anger or upset. I certainly felt emotional and upset initially, but the more I did my affirmations, the better I felt. The affirmation of the day became a source of comfort and support as I adjusted to making affirmations a part of my morning routine.

My number one takeaway from this challenge is that an affirmation a day keeps my stress away! Through affirmations, I have gained confidence, become more aware of my capabilities, and learned to appreciate the little things that make me happy.

One area where I still need to focus on and improve is attaching objectives or actions to the affirmations. Otherwise, I may remain a passive procrastinator. I realise the importance of intentionality to ensure I don't stay stagnant but actually move forward and achieve results. This is something I am committed to working on in August.

Looking back, I am committed to continuing my affirmation journey. I have experienced the tremendous benefits of taking time for myself, relaxing, reflecting, and living the best life I can create. I no longer feel guilty. Thank you, affirmations!

I am sincerely grateful for the opportunity the 30 Days of Affirmations Challenge provided. It has helped me view my life through different lenses. I can now reframe any negativity into an upbeat and positive perspective. I can breathe, affirm, smile, and live.

Life feels so good!

Mandi's 30 Days of Affirmations

1. I am committed to being kind and patient with myself when I am struggling with technology and workload.
2. I am committed to feeling positive today and strong.
3. I am committed to feeling confident and calm in all I do.
4. I am grateful that I am reframing situations so that I don't feel negative or stressed. I have the qualities to handle these uncomfortable situations.
5. I am committed to being positive despite the challenges I face.
6. I am committed to taking time out for me.
7. I am grateful for my special 'me' time which helps me heal.
8. I am committed to feeling restful and I am grateful for my relaxing surroundings.
9. I am so grateful that I am me. No one can take me away.
10. I am committed to taking all the time that I need for me to feel energised.
11. I am grateful for the love and support of my family and friends.
12. I am grateful for the peacefulness that I can create with relaxation.
13. I am committed to being strong and resilient. I am grateful that I have these qualities to protect myself.

14. I give myself permission to heal and I am grateful that I can heal.

15. I am committed to forgiving those loved ones that hurt me.

16. I am grateful for the calm and peace. I look forward to the day ahead.

17. I am committed to celebrating all that is me.

18. I am committed to bringing more focus and structure to my day.

19. I am grateful for the simple things in life that make me appreciate being alive—the warmth of the sun, the smell of the woods, the breeze through my bones and just being in that moment.

20. I feel joy in all that I do and all that I achieve.

21. I am grateful for my doggy run today as I saw 2 hares in the fields.

22. I am committed to completing three tasks that are important to me: my expenses, my pension, and five minutes of meditation.

23. I am grateful for the peace and calm that I am creating this month.

24. I am committed to living the best life that I can.

25. I am grateful for new friends and communities.

26. I am grateful that I am finding forgiveness in my heart as I continue on this journey.

27. I am fearless and will continue to focus on my achievements, however small or large.

28. I am committed to doing my best today.

29. I am joyous about the future that I am creating.

30. I am focused and grateful for all the positives that happen during my day.

Catherine

My general feeling about the affirmation challenge is overwhelmingly positive.

Previously, whenever I woke up after a bad night's sleep, or feeling unwell (which to be honest was most days) my first thoughts were negative — how tired I am, how much pain and discomfort I'm in. How am I going to get through the day? I wish I could go back to bed. But throughout the challenge, I woke each day in anticipation — what's going to be my positive thought today? How good do I feel when I read out my affirmation? But most of all, how grateful I am for my life. And how calm I feel.

I automatically switched up the negative feelings for one of acceptance. Even though I'm tired/unwell, I accept my situation and feel calm and grateful for my life.

As the days progressed, this became easier and easier. I automatically began each day with deep breaths and a body stretch. I smiled. I relaxed. A much better way to start the day and this also affected my attitude throughout the day.

Now I have a 'bank' of 30 affirmations, I'm going to choose one each morning to repeat. I feel so very grateful to have found this new way to start each day. And I've also found myself using them throughout the day, perhaps when I have an argument with someone or feel stressed at work. And on a macro level, I've started applying the affirmations to my

future. I can change my life, take decisions that are good for me. Move forwards.

I think I will always use affirmations. Such a simple tool, but I can't imagine starting the day without one!

I've also shared my list with some close friends – they can use them if they wish, or just learn more about me and support my new positive outlook.

I kept a diary across the 30 days and it's interesting to see how I used, and then relied upon the affirmation of the day. I had good days and bad days but it was interesting to see how I reacted. How I remained calm. I've really enjoyed spending time reading

books to distract me and having long, relaxing baths in the evening. Just lying there and thinking and breathing. Such a simple thing to do, but so effective.

Catherine's Diary

Day 2 . I woke feeling very calm and contented. Slept well.

Day 3. I slept well and felt calm. Had a long bath last night, which is something I never do - usually, it's really quick. Lay in the bath reading a book. Totally relaxed.

Day 4. I awoke feeling unwell and spent much of the day resting.

But remained contented. Read a book to distract any negative

thoughts.

Day 5. I woke early feeling rested.

Day 6. I found myself enjoying doing chores! I took my time and thought to myself that it was good exercise.

Day 7. I'm enjoying early morning walks rather than being irritated that I am the one who always takes the dog out.

Day 8. Woken up at 5am by the dog which would usually annoy me. I really didn't mind! I just accepted the situation and thought, oh well, I can sleep tonight.

Day 9. Woke early. Decided to give myself permission to be lazy and have a restful day. Previously I would have felt bad about this, but I just enjoyed it.

Day 10. Slept badly with stressful dreams. Usually, this would impact my entire day. But I just took it in my stride because I'm so grateful to be me.

Day 11. I was unwell in the night but just accepted it and didn't get angry. I remained calm. I didn't get upset. This is a huge change and great progress.

Day 12. I'm exhausted but accepting of my physical condition. Looking forwards rather than constantly questioning why I feel so tired.

Day 13-17. On holiday - most rested for years! A simple family holiday to Norfolk. But it was one of the best holidays I've ever had. I felt so incredibly relaxed and grateful.

Day 18,19. Starting to think about the end of my holiday and back to work/life stress. Will aim to bring my holiday vibe back home. The sound of the sea is SO relaxing. Will definitely return.

Day 20. Home today but we both said this was the best UK holiday we've had - so relaxing and peaceful. Time to think. Make decisions. Visualise the future. Reassess our lives. Focus on what is truly important and above all, be grateful.

Day 21. Slept badly. Woke feeling unwell. But instead of being annoyed (as usual) I am grateful for each day - regardless of how I feel physically.

Day 22. A difficult day with work and frustrating admin. Rather than getting upset and stressed, I went for a walk and really managed to calm down quickly.

Day 23. A difficult evening. Didn't sleep. Woke up exhausted but determined to move on in a positive way.

Day 25. Bad news from the doctor really brought me down. But I feel tired rather than stressed. Working on acceptance.

Day 26. Acceptance, positivity and being kind to myself. Time to move on with a positive mindset.

Day 27. Awoke feeling rubbish. Breathed deeply and welcomed the day!

Day 29. Slept well. Awoke feeling grateful and (unlike me) not feeling anxious about the hot weather.

Day 30. Awoke with a sense of achievement at having reached 30 days. Although I was quite unwell yesterday, I slept well, woke early and drove to the beach.

If I had to sum up my challenge it would be this:

My life, my decisions, my rules.

My life is in my hands - don't waste a single day being negative or down however you feel.

Accept that each week will have ups and downs – celebrate and feel grateful for the good times and work on acceptance of the bad.

Let go of people and thoughts that don't support the positive.

Start each day afresh with a deep breath and a smile.

Catherine's 30 Days of Affirmations

1. I am grateful for all that I have, each and every day.
2. I don't need validation from my peers. I know my own achievements. I am enough.
3. I feel positive about the future. A whole new chapter awaits.
4. I accept that pain and discomfort are part of my life, part of me, but I do not ever let this overwhelm me.
5. I respect my body and listen to it. I use my energy wisely.
6. I welcome each day with a smile. I'm happy to be here!
7. I am grateful for the calm in my life.
8. I am committed to making the most of each day on this beautiful earth.
9. I am a positive person. There is no place for negativity in my life.
10. I don't waste my time being envious of other people - their energy, their success - because that is them and I am me.
11. I accept that my relationship with my parents is complex and I value my time with them.
12. I breathe deeply and remember how lucky I am.
13. I view Fatigue as an old friend, rather than a new enemy.
14. I deserve to be relaxed and happy.

15. I am so grateful for all that I have and all that I am.

16. I am worthy of the love and respect that I receive from family and friends.

17. The path I am on is the right one. I feel an abundance of calm.

18. Today is a good day. I'm grateful for each good day and I will hold on to the memory of this feeling.

19. I deserve happiness.

20. I am committed to living a simpler life. Where love and contentment are all that I need.

21. I feel an abundance of calm and I share this with those around me.

22. I celebrate each day and I'm so grateful to be here!

23. I am moving forwards - heading towards new goals. I welcome new challenges with open arms!

24. I let go of thoughts that do not serve me. Pffffft! And they are gone!

25. I am so proud of myself - of all that I have achieved and of the person I have become.

26. I accept my illness but I am not defined by it. There is no place in my life for negativity!

27. I begin each day by breathing deeply and feeling content.

28. The next stage in my life is exciting and new. I deserve this.

29. I let go of people and places that hold me back.

30. I see a hill and I climb it. Because it feels better to be at the top.

Shirley Ann Felder

As I sit here and reflect upon the last 30 days, I am in awe of myself and my coach. If I'm being honest, sometimes, in the past, the affirmations felt like something just to say, even though I was taught over 25 years ago that the most powerful things that we will ever hear are what comes after "I am."

Being aware of oneself and knowing what to do after you realize why you're feeling the way you feel and the origin of those thoughts leaves room for the healing process to begin. "WOW," is all I can say. I am grateful for the process that I have been taught and for the practice of creating my affirmations. I appreciate that through this practice, I really feel the positive changes in my thinking and the benefits of taking time for myself to breathe, sit silent, scan my body, and then express what all of that felt like or brought up.

Now the magic comes when I can reframe what I call stinking thinking, self-limiting beliefs, and their sabotaging thoughts and actions into I AM statements that move me spiritually.

I must admit that I wanted to join this challenge because I felt like I would be able to collect some knowledge about the different modalities, meditation, moving my body and that positive thinking stuff. I figured I could add this knowledge to my coaching structure to help my clients. What I received was so much more. What I realized is that I needed to put my mask on first so that I can help my clients even more. I learned that there were some things in my way that I could take back control of and not give that old flippant attitude to. I realized one of the things that really was holding me back was my fear of success.

I shared with my groups and friends and clients that I work with what I was doing so that they would cheer me on, support me, join in, and prevent me from quitting because typically, I quit things when it gets challenging. I realize that even with all the work that I do on stinking thinking, I still have some stinking thinking, and I know it's human, but still. I joined this challenge because I thought I would learn something, but I learned many things, mostly about myself. I learned that I am smart enough. I learned that I had been successful before, and it took a lot of dedication and sacrifice not to mention the pressure. If I went all in that would mean I'd have all the pressure, stress, public opinion and so on. No time for me. I've come to enjoy this "just enough" lifestyle, so I told myself. I also learned there were some secondary benefits that I was holding on to that were truly cancerous, just eating away at me slowly, but I held onto them because there was at least a little benefit in it for me, even if unhealthy.

I have since joined this challenge and realized that I must be aware of the things that no longer serve me, I must accept and trust my feelings and myself, and I must continually take action. I've recently earned the largest speaking contract I've ever had. I've had three comedic proposals. I am an author of two collaborative book projects. I am staying in action. I am taking steps every day towards my dream of being an international motivational speaker and coach. I designed a full-year coaching program to launch in September. Taking the steps to be aware and take action has led to tangible progress toward my dreams.

This stuff wasn't taught in my home. I just started to learn about it in my late 20's, but it still didn't feel like it could really happen for me, for us. I went through the motions and taught it, but I didn't internalize it. Now that I know more and have a better understanding, I put together a daily ritual. I allowed myself time to sit and not feel guilty. I put some boundaries in place, and I have shared with other people what I was about to commit to. It became believable and achievable because things were happening. I was in motion taking action. That is why representation is important because it allows us to believe that there are people like us who are making a difference, and we begin to see that we can too.

I joined this challenge because I had made a connection with someone who looked like me and my family members but approached life in a completely different way. When I heard him a year ago, I realized that I have heard this stuff before but never like this. I come from the old school "fake it 'til you make it," and I often use the analogy of how we used to have the bag phone and now we have a smartphone, and I believe that's the same case here. What used to work doesn't anymore, and we grow as we stretch ourselves. After hearing him, I started to believe it could really apply to me. So, I listened and paid close attention because, "When we know better, we can do better." I've learned the power of breathwork. I've learned the power of telling myself the truth, how I really feel, and then being able to have a true conversation with myself, "Is it real? Is this made up? Is it really my destiny? Am I really NOT enough, smart, pretty, dark and any other "not" thought for that moment? Absolutely not! I am, as I still recall being taught.

I also never thought about the boundaries or the importance of the environment growing up as a young child around insanity. You tend to look at it as, "Oh, it's just a part of life." However, that's really not the case, and we can do so much better. I was grateful. I was good with awareness. I wasn't good at asking for help. I could do a lot better with my health and moving my body and being able to sit still on some days and do nothing without feeling guilty. The pandemic helped me out a great deal, however, there is still much work to be done.

At this stage of my life, I know my core values. I know my purpose is to use my humor to deliver authentic messages to motivate and inspire people to love themselves and treat others with much-needed self-love and respect. I know that because I am unlike anyone else and that is my gift. I know this because I am a burst of loving energy and I believe in me. I know that I am necessary, and I am valuable. I know that I am exactly where I'm supposed to be. I affirm that my voice matters, and my smile is powerful.

Most importantly, I recognize the power of my gift, skills, and experience and I accept what comes with that. My values of being authentic and making a difference mean everything to me. Someone's made a difference in mine, so that is my mission. So, I will continue to work daily on being aware of my feelings and surroundings and being grateful for the many opportunities. I am willing to accept my truth and I will continue to stay in motion including adding a little something terror-exciting every now and then.

“Knowing others is intelligence — knowing yourself is true wisdom.

Mastering others is strength — Mastering yourself is true power.”

Shirley's 30 Days of Affirmations

1. I am committed to creating daily rituals.
2. I am committed to unearthing my greatness.
3. I am committed to moving my body more.
4. I am worthy of the same energy and effort that I give to others.
5. I am opening up to being able to ask for help more often.
6. I am committed to learning how to just be still when my body tells me to and not feel guilty about not doing more.
7. I am giving myself permission to be loved. I've had walls up for many years. Today I let them down.
8. I am grateful for the relationships I have created and nurtured on Clubhouse over the last year.
9. I am committed to this process and my dreams.
10. I am worthy of the opportunities I attract.
11. I am grateful for another year on this planet, and I give myself some grace and love. As today I turn a sexy 56.
12. I am grateful for my ability to create loving, trusting authentic and meaningful relationships with purpose and intention. As yesterday was my birthday and over 20+ women showed up to pay such beautiful respect and tribute to me my work and my purpose on this planet. It was a beautiful feeling to know you make a difference in people's lives. Today feeling blessed, humbled and grateful.
13. I am grateful for having my ships in order. relationships, worships, entrepreneurships, hardships and ownerships.
14. I am committed to continually finding ways to love and accept my physical attributes as is and share them with

Mother Nature. I find myself emerging empowered and very creative.

15. I am grateful for my courage to share my dreams with others out loud.
16. I am strong and courageous, and I can do anything I put my mind to.
17. I am exactly where I'm supposed to be.
18. I recognize the power of my skills and experiences, and I accept what comes with that.
19. I am committed to nurturing that funny little girl inside of me more often.
20. I am grateful for my ability to know how and when to reset.
21. I am going to start trusting in my own knowing.
22. I am an amazing burst of loving energy and I believe in me.
23. I am necessary and I am valuable.
24. I am grateful for and worthy of the love of my tribe.
25. I affirm that my voice matters and my smile is powerful.
26. I am committed to staying in motion and action.
27. I already have the skills and tools I need to see my dreams through.
28. I am committed to introducing my body to all types of nourishment and care.
29. I am unlike anyone else and that is my best gift.
30. I am committed to collecting tools and grace for me to win this race.

Daniella V Robbins

What made you join the challenge?

I experienced heartbreak for the first time September 2021, spiralling into a sense of losing myself, having never been in love before or in a relationship with a male of high-intensity connection. I felt a pure and genuine appreciation, love and respect from another, besides my self-love. I lost a man whom I could trust wholeheartedly, even when based between country borders, a pandemic of travel restrictions and at a distance - he enabled me to surpass any childhood construct of believing that romantic love relations are highly likely to encounter infidelity and more so, made me believe in the possibility to love again and reconnect with a like-minded human being, who champions loyalty and exchanges speaking of pure love. With feeling an absolute loss of self and self-joy post-breakup, my lifetime habit of self-sufficiency to sort feelings did not apply and I acknowledged the need to find tools, in order to manage my heartbreak and overcome this sense of loss. At the time my body also manifested physically with abnormal hair loss, deepening my lack of control and setting up self-resistance towards a new me.

Before you started what were you struggling with the most?

Before starting EFT and the 30 Days of Affirmations Challenge, I was understanding that my core had shifted and that I was behaving out of my norm. From my body being tightened at all times, carrying a sense of weight pressed on my chest to streaming tears, on the cross-trainer at the gym, whilst listening to power music on my playlist titled "When you can't escape the truth", which I curated during my deepest moment of grief post-breakup, as a way of expressing this loss.

I would randomly cry in front and behind the camera on a virtual call of 200+ employees, as well as confront high procrastination, all in all slowing my ability to complete priority tasks, furthering the sense of losing myself and muting my high-performance profile. When reflecting, there was a perception of self-sabotage when I interpreted my behaviours or reactions to be misaligned with my values, or with "the girl I once knew".

I recognised that I had to radically accept my ex-partner is part of my present, as a series of historical moments that have broken me down and evolved me to build something beyond what I know existed. On the one hand, I was a person who lived with self-joy prior to that relationship, however, post-relationship I felt that not only had I naturally lost the joy shared with my partner, but also extracted my own self-joy and deeply struggled with that reality. On the other hand, I have been holding onto the inner recurring vision that he is the love of my life, father to "our" future children and an opportunity lost, to create life with someone who I still feel mirrors my values and desire to build a sustainable family unit & progress humanity, together, even though the truth is that he was not equipped to be my "right now". I progressively acknowledged that I have evolved, pre-during-post relationship and needed to now identify emotional weights, in order to move forward with the desperate want to find self-joy again.

Where are you now with the challenges you were facing?

I can push through walls of blue and walk with joy & sunshine.

This affirmation on Day 16 of the 30 Days of Affirmation Challenge, truly represents the transformation this process has enabled me to experience. If I am to visualise this experience thus far that's how I would illustrate it, pushing a wall of blues, sadness and absence, whilst cohabiting with new joyful moments, a new sense of self and transformed energy (without him). The heartbreak remains, however, I am proactively seeking new ways to find self-joy and understand the gravity points of my relationship. Breathing body compressions and visualisation with colour-coded emotions, allow me to relive the gravity moments, be honest with my inner self and move to reduce and release their intense emotion and convert them into affirmations. As an external impact, this process has seasoned me to talking more openly about my feelings and the break up with my closest, expressing beyond sadness and utilising breathing techniques to complete my expression and gradually lessen my frequency of showing up and breaking down into tears. I do believe now that I am living out the motto of a generation, "It's OK not to be OK", alongside a potential life-long learning practice of emotional measurement and evaluation, to truly be unlocked, gain clarity of what I strive for and grow to be my true self at peace for self-joy.

What was the hardest thing about being consistent with the challenge?

I am grateful to have learnt the ability to be disciplined beyond my profession during this challenge, for my personal gain. The hardest part of this process I wish to share is when your feelings reflect yesterday's very closely and you do not hold a sense of progress. One may try to find alternative words to reframe those emotions and honour expressing a state of blueness, but there is at times an inner ego voice denying your vulnerability and highlighting this to lack merit and blur your clarity. I say do your best to manage your energy, avoid distractions and simply keep going and try again to find balance.

What three things did you enjoy the most about the experience?

I have savoured waking up daily with an intentional conversation with myself to raise self-awareness, reflecting on the previous day's events, recalling dreams of the night before, spotting the emotional triggers, patterns and moods developed. I am an advocate of sharing the revelations of the process, whether that be with strangers or your closest to set yourself free. The Challenge has created a safe space for me to apply EFT tools daily, with the commitment to share consistently for 30 days in a monitored environment.

What was your number one takeaway?

My number one takeaway is how to practice the importance of unearthing daily emotions, function with better clarity and intentionally seek self-joy. It has been a guided journey to learn to go from just feeling, to practising going in deep on myself and identifying one takeaway that can be reframed into an affirmation and followed up as an actionable insight.

If you could go back in time, what would you say to yourself before the challenge knowing what you know now?

I would tell my younger self, that only you hold the potential to empower yourself and to elevate your situation into light, when you commit to your well-being, going deep and consistently owning your affirmations. You will be excited for the future as you live to prioritise your heart's desires and not conform to the new norm. You will vibrate highly and surround yourself with joyous power sources that serve you.

Daniella's 30 Days of Affirmations

1. I am committed to being consistently proactive to experience joy whilst listening to my body.
2. I am committed to my well-being to find self-joy again.
3. I am grateful for the loving friendships I am surrounded by and for becoming at peace with myself.
4. I rise restless. I am committed to being more disciplined with what is new for me to own, facing procrastination and discarding the worry of former responsibilities.
5. I am hopeful and optimistic for joyful moments.
6. I am committed to being consistently proactive to experience joy whilst listening to my body.
7. I am committed to the process of letting go and believing in self-peace for self-joy.
8. I am committed to being at peace with the world and exercising self-validation.
9. I am grateful for the simple things that bring me joy and I am committed to exploring myself for new ones to be energised.
10. I rise to feel self-love and stay committed to building stronger connections with others.
11. I am tolerant of high vulnerability to transform forward.
12. I am grateful for the outlet music gives me in life and will always prioritise music to unlock my true self.

13. I am committed to being kinder to my body so good habits are not broken.

14. I am at peace with myself and celebrate who I am today - strong, proactive, kind, independent and confident in challenging the norm.

15. I am feeling joyful and grateful for committing to the daily affirmations process that centres me to tune in with my core and reframe my inner thoughts. My output to the world remains positive with clarity of what I strive for, to find self-joy again.

16. I have joy for myself even without you.

17. I can push through walls of blue and walk with joy & sunshine.

18. I am committed to facing you in my dreams and transmit joy and pain in order to walk with a sense of relief.

19. I am committed to sharing my truth with my closest and finding joy in the comfort of being heard and loved.

20. I am committed to not living in the past yet desire to champion the comforts and power moments that made me thrive in order to not forget what joy can feel like with another.

21. I must manage my energy regardless of disappointing others.

22. I champion living with high vibrations and not engaging with those that do not serve me.

23. I move with purpose and I am empowered by others that do so also.

24. I am committed to self-care in order to help others I want to see win.

25. I am light to others in moments of darkness and it is my self-joy that illuminates me.

26. I am focused on completing this week with a high sense of achievement.

27. I am grateful for my fearless spontaneity and ability to find and bring joy to myself & others.

28. I am committed to meditation for balance of thought.

29. I rise with a sense of independence and self-care.

30. I am joyous for myself first and then as a reminder for others that life can be self-fulfilling.

Masia One

What made you join the challenge?

Trust for Spoon: Having checked out the app, I found the approach to be inspiring and a really positive way to start the day.

Curiosity: I have not participated in a group like this before.

Before you started what were you struggling with the most?

Clarity for the path ahead: My life has been unexpectedly uprooted in the last 2 years having been stuck in Malaysia, then making the decision to stay here. As such I continue to pursue musical work but looking at the possibility to pursue an island jerk shack dream and have the confidence to step into that world having been in the music industry for 20 years and knowing very little about F&B.

Where are you now with the challenges you were facing?

2 weeks ago, following recovery from Covid and cold, I came into a really negative space where I was listening to a lot of doubts, destructive self-talk and fears in my mind, which is uncharacteristic for someone that usually jumps off a cliff and figures out the details later. I continued the affirmations throughout but didn't feel the same conviction and enthusiasm that I came into the space with.

What was the hardest thing about being consistent with the challenge?

When circumstances are good and there is time and space, I lean into the affirmations being thoughtful about what I want to share for myself and taking time to meditate, dream and think deeper. On days where I was feeling very negative, stressed or claustrophobic, I felt like I was spewing forward cliches and didn't feel affirmed in my affirmations.

What three things did you enjoy the most about the experience?

1. Taking time to stop the noise and practice the art of listening to an inner self.
2. The challenge of consistency to push forward, on good days and bad.
3. The group setting gave me perspective that everyone has their own world's where they face their own challenges. This allowed me to step back from my own issues and see the bigger picture, that we are all just moving through life and figuring it out.

What was your number one takeaway?

Affirmations aren't just a wish or dream to write on a piece of paper and believe it will manifest. I enjoyed that you shared with us a way to take the time and space for the mind before writing the personal affirmation with purpose and clarity.

If you could go back in time, what would you say to yourself before the challenge knowing what you know now?

Share more with the group. I went through a time of wanting to really self-isolate and didn't want to participate - but once I returned to the group felt regretful that I didn't enjoy the full experience with a collective all working toward a shared personal goal.

Masia's 30 Days of Affirmations

July 3 Communication: No matter if I do not see eye-to-eye with my loved ones, communication and voicing what our needs are, will help grow the understanding, patience and bonds that are held. I aspire to work on better communication, not for who's wrong or right but to forge deeper and more meaningful connections.

July 4 Friendship: Meet and connect with genuine friends and people to grow meaningful and fulfilling relationships to help the road ahead.

July 5 Roadtrip: As I hit the open road, I'm open to new opportunities that fall in line with the move to Langkawi or wherever the right foundation to build is.

July 6 Balance: May I understand deeper the perfect balance between give and take.

July 7: Restful time is not time that is wasted but rather focused on healing, emptying and rejuvenating. I welcome this restful time that will lead to a clear mind for better decisions and life choices made.

July 8: Plans might change, but Jah will always provide. I trust the process.

July 9: Celebrating the time and ability to write and sing a gillion songs and grateful for this well of inspiration that replenishes. I welcome the ability to create and be stable financially and sustainably doing the thing that brings so much joy.

July 10: While the moon is waning I plan. So that when the light is full we can celebrate as a creative community. I ask for clarity, consistency and the patience to plan and organize for myself and the artists on my label toward shared success.

July 11: Manifesting international ties between the islands of SE Asia and the world. I feel blessed that I may be given the opportunity and remuneration to be this conduit.

July 12: I affirm to stay present, yet cherish memories with passion and fondness.

July 13: Helping others find success with their music is a joy. I see the work done to return to the label Nusantara Records 100 fold - in financial remuneration, in relationships built and in growing a positive reputation. Working together we will succeed.

July 14: As I find my way, I ask for clarity to balance music and new aspirations for Suka Suka Sauce. I know my way is not necessarily THE way, and so I relax my mind, trust the universe and give way to something better than I could imagine.

July 15: As negative, angry and doubtful emotions overwhelm me, I know there is a reason why these thoughts are coming up now. I affirm patience with myself to go through the process and learn, grow and evolve.

July 16: I envision a wedding in the near future to share the love I have found to be blessed by friends, family and loved ones.

July 17: I seek investment for the new projects and more importantly the right team. I open myself to connect with the right people.

July 18: To stop fighting with myself, I reframe my situation and emotions. I ask for a deeper understanding of these emotions.

July 19: I will be kinder to myself.

July 20: I found my driver's license after losing it for 1 year! I see some road trips for hubby and Zendog in the future and am excited for this newfound freedom it brings.

July 21: I have dedicated 20 years of my life to the music business. As I move toward working smarter rather than harder, I see the reason for my life's journey to soon show itself as the path opens.

July 22: I will give more love, time, energy, patience and little acts of care to my husband, to fall in love over and over with this blessing and not take him for granted.

July 23: It's ok to hide and rest. I ask that this quiet time brings the healing that is needed.

July 24: Ipoh, Penang or Langkawi (or all of the above?), I ask for the answers to reveal themselves as I do the research necessary for the finding of a dream - Suka Suka Jamaican Jerk Shack in SE Asia.

July 25: I ask for the patience to teach, and the ability to say no to the things that do not serve this path to a nourishing way.

July 26: I ask for the bravery to say yes to the right opportunities as I feel myself changing.

July 27: Waterfalls are cleansing and a glimpse into the importance of nature as part of my everyday life. I beckon the life that stays connected with root, ground, tree, clean food, fresh air, sunshine, smiling faces and laughter, and the foundation to hold it all.

July 28: New moon arises as we prepare to release "Blood Moon" for Trinidadian artists Blufyah and Jahwise. I see this single and it's remixes going far and finding a sync placement in the most unexpected places.

July 29: I am loved, I am appreciated, I am safe.

July 30: As I reflect on affirmations in the last month, I think about the re-occurring themes that come up: I see a future with clarity, wisdom, nature, creativity, meaningful relationships and connections, time & space to care for self, financial freedom, stability, and a balance between helping myself and others. May I trust the process and keep on this divine path I have been blessed with.

Valerie Paul-Kerry

I was in a position of limbo. I felt stuck and was trying to make sense of my feelings and where I was. My mother had recently died and I got married all within 2 months. It was expected and I went away for two weeks and had a lovely honeymoon. But I was still (and currently) trying to process all that happened to me. Two major shifts in my life and beneath all of that was my calling for acting. Then Elroy reached out to me to join. I didn't really know what to expect and to be honest I didn't really take everything in, on what we had to do, but I didn't hesitate as I felt without hesitation that this was going to help me.

My mum had dementia and she had carers, but me being the youngest and only daughter, I was her main carer. I was doing this whilst working full time, looking after two children (although now two young adults) maintaining a relationship and trying to follow my dream and passion of acting. My self-worth is what I struggled with the most. It is something I have struggled with most of my life. A constant battle of telling myself I am worthy, but society, environment, people and relationships often suffocate me into giving in to negative thoughts. Repeating old behaviour patterns, listening to the wrong people with their jealousy, negativity. Being an open book to people who in turn would rip open my pages for their satisfaction. People pleasing to try and heal my wound or ease attacks of feeling guilty.

When I was younger I was told to be quiet, to not have an opinion, just be good. I never felt seen or heard. I was constantly looking for validation in my life. When my confidence was knocked I thought this was normal and to be expected as it is what I deserved. I just wanted to be me and speak my truth. My mother had installed a fear and control in me that I believed was true. When I wanted to break out of this condition, the voice in my head would always bring me back to what I believed was true, that I was unworthy, my voice did not matter, and I should only be seen but not heard.

The one-to-one was invaluable as that was the catalyst for the opening of the truth. I always knew it, but actually coming face to face with it and saying it out loud, helped me not be afraid and realise it is not my belief but my mother's fear that she passed onto me. Confronting memories was very painful and very very scary. Doing the initial work made the course much easier to understand and go through. Knowing that I could overcome these thoughts and emotions was a revelation. The exercise of talking out loud is very powerful as it helped me recognise that I have a voice and I matter.

The challenges are still very much here, but they do not linger for as long as they used to. Acknowledging how I feel, and accepting how I feel allows me to then take action. I can choose to stay in the same place or I can shift. Sometimes I stay and let the feeling soak through as I feel it has to and I am ok with that. Other times I let the feeling hover and do not allow it to soak through. The main thing is recognising what I feel and allowing myself to feel it. Pausing, breathing and talking out loud are all tactics that help me shift from the difficult challenges. Recognising when I need rest and being kind to myself was unheard of before, but now I do not feel guilty when I need to put those things in place. Spending a whole month focusing on me has been a new shift for me. Guilt would always creep in and force me back to old behaviours until my body forces me to rest. I now manage me better.

What was the hardest thing about being consistent with the challenge? It was definitely making time for yourself. The old behaviours of putting everything else first, and prioritising me last was very hard. I had to get into a routine which was taking the time as soon as I woke up. I found it became much easier to listen to your body and depending on the events that occurred the connection with how you were feeling was much easy to recognise. Whereas there were times dealing with certain people would put my back up, and make me angry, I was actually able to step back and see behaviour as their issue and not mine. I didn't hold on to that feeling for as long as I would have. The times where I did not make time for myself, the day was a mess and things that happened I had no control over as my mind was not set from the beginning of the day. The affirmations are like a protection, a force field that only you know the combination and the answer. Having this secret with me is very satisfying!

What three things did you enjoy the most about the experience?

For me, it was taking time for myself. Not having to explain anything to anyone. Working out how I feel and being comfortable with that was something that I have done as a luxury. When I have been too tired with doing everything and the only thing I can do is nothing! Which is usually when I am sick!

Being able to write down my feelings and turn them into something positive instead of spending time fighting and thinking and talking about '*what I don't*'. Turning those thoughts into things that I do want was a very hard challenge as it is so easier to put down the negative feelings as that is what we have been trained to do.

Being part of the group and sharing our triumphs and acknowledging and lifting each other. Being part of and amongst people who are on the same energy frequency is very powerful. The support of each other and understanding each other's pain was invaluable. It is surprising as I was very apprehensive at first as I wasn't sure if people would be open, but allowing to trust you and the process has been a wonderful experience.

I went with my gut to begin the course and it has served immensely. Knowing me closer is proof that I can continue to be a better person and the person I wish to be. Taking time for myself, no matter what form is a must that has to be done daily. I know the benefits that it has given me and I know the loss it will cause if I do not commit. The work you put in gives you the result you deserve. I have proven to myself being kind to me gives me such rewarding results.

If you could go back in time, what would you say to yourself before the challenge, knowing what you know now?

Do not be AFRAID!!! This is a course that allows you to really feel and then turn your feelings into positive thoughts to help you in your everyday life. It may be hard in the beginning and you may not fully understand what is happening but go with it! Things become clearer and easier. It is a blessing to allow time to be with you. Painful things will come up, but like life, uncomfortable things pass. The thing is focusing on YOU and what matters to YOU. You will have support from your group which is a wonderful group of people who support, lift and encourage you. You can reach out anytime and have a one to one. The is an exercise to benefit you and give you tools to reach your full potential.

Affirmations can accompany your meditation, exercise and diet. It can be used in conjunction with all of those things, but it definitely has to remain part of everyday practice. This is an exercise that takes very little time and can be done whilst lying down in bed, anywhere where you can be quiet for a short while. It forces you to quiet the mind and listen to yourself. It is quick and easy. For me, it is a good start to the day like the breakfast of mindfulness before you begin your exercises. Putting your mindset first is the best start to the day and a way of life next to breathing.

Valerie's 30 Days of Affirmations

1. I am recognising my limits and allowing myself to pause.
2. I am ready to be bold and face the challenges presented to move me forward in my passion.
3. I am keeping sight of the vision I want.
4. I am protecting the light inside me, my flame shines bright.
5. I am courageous and strong, my voice and views matter.
6. I am full of creativity and allow it to flow freely.
7. I am giving myself permission to be present and enjoy the experience.
8. I am able to listen to myself and make decisions that are right for me.
9. I am ready to accept the abundance of joy the universe is giving to me.
10. I am eager for the lessons life provides and to learn from them so I can move confidently forward.
11. I am grounded in my truth.
12. I am pausing to embrace the part of unknowingness in me.
13. I am being kind to my mind and body and give it the rest and nourishment it deserves.
14. I embrace my life and elevate in the joy presented.
15. I accept the past but choose to live in the present.
16. I am balanced and at peace with myself.

17. I give myself permission to say no and feel no guilt.

18. I am changing my lifestyle to suit me.

19. I am good at my job, and with my skills, knowledge and resilience I am enjoying the process of stepping further towards my goal.

20. I am protecting my space and my boundaries.

21. I love honesty and deeply make no excuses for it.

22. I am allowing myself to receive the joy presented to me.

23. I am putting myself first and restoring my energy.

24. I believe in me and acknowledge the signs to help me trust the process.

25. I choose to make choices that empower me.

26. I am continuing with the flow and not resisting.

27. I celebrate me and my achievements of how far I have come.

28. I am slowing down and listening... To be more aware.

29. I am grateful for my past and the great achievers that are with me every step of the way.

30. I am a warrior. My strengths and resilience take action when needed.

31. I am a winner because I believe in my truth.

Cat

What made you join the course?

Gratitude for Spoon's influence in my life

Before you started what were you struggling with the most?

Not before this class, so much, but before encountering these concepts, I struggled to take time away from family members I help care for at home.

What did you believe was the root cause of the struggle?

My own confusion and internal conflict.

How did you learn about your past struggles from doing the course?

I worked through a good chunk of my internal conflict and brought things into better alignment. I continue to work on more, and expect it will always be needed, but the backlog is less overwhelming, since I am less dramatically out of alignment, because I'm keeping up with it daily.

Where are you now with the challenges you were facing?

On track

What was the hardest thing about being consistent with the challenge?

Taking the time

What three things did you enjoy the most about the experience?

Reading affirmations in the group, accessing my inner guidance and power and thinking through the prompts to answer them.

What was your number one takeaway?

Stay in the ring. Your strengths are equal to your challenges if you appreciate them, leverage them, and flex them intentionally every day.

If you could go back in time, what would you say to yourself before the challenge knowing what you now know?

You are gonna love this. Don't even worry about putting the time in. It will be a pleasure.

How can you now use affirmations as part of your mindfulness practice?

Speak them to myself daily. Write them. Mean them.

Cat's 30 Days of Affirmations

1. I arise to the wonder of a new day in safety. I anticipate joy.
2. I accept the grace that arrives in my life. I am committed to enjoying fully.
3. I claim my power and embrace my responsibility. I let the sun within me warm my heart, burn through my blockages, and blaze out to the world. I love my own strength and shine without apology. I thankfully affirm my right and power to make choices that serve me.
4. I love myself where I am today and stay with myself in friendship as I continue to make my path.
5. I am the ground I build on. I am firm in my truth, and I trust myself. I make space and silence to find my bedrock.
6. I grow at my own pace. Without force or hindrance, I blossom in my time.
7. At my core, I am perfect, pure, and connected to all through my essential being. This is unalterable.
8. I feel the depth and strength of my roots, and I choose to flower boldly. I know I can risk delicate, vulnerable, passing blossoms. I have the resources to create them over and over.
9. I give myself permission to savor life in every moment.
10. I purposefully practice equanimity and soak in contentment. I pause and allow these qualities to saturate my soul and seep into the marrow of my bones.

11. I treat myself with kindness and respect.

12. I let possibilities come play with me as my friends. I welcome them to come and go, while I stay open and observe

13. I use my energy wisely; I respect both ebbs and flows.

14. I notice the beauty, benefits, and blessings in my life. I linger on what's good.

15. I cherish my enthusiasm. I feed that which feeds me, and I honor my joy.

16. I am the lead architect in my life, working with the raw materials available to create structures that support my thriving.

17. I value what I have and my gratitude is wealth.

18. I show up for myself; I take care of myself, and I know I deserve my own love.

19. I commit to the ongoing effort it takes to keep steering my life in the direction I desire. I train my intentions in order to realize them.

20. I catch my moment.

21. My steps are steady and purposeful.

22. I celebrate what I *am* able to do.

23. I embrace the spirit of play and experiment every day.

24. There is nothing that I have to do. I allow love to reveal itself to me in endless guises. I *choose* total engagement with my life's unfolding.

25. I take time to make time.

26. I meet myself with friendly respect, curiosity, and non-resistance. I am open to learning from myself and all my experiences.

27. I relish my good times and luxuriate in the love that is in my life. I feel it fully.

28. I can roll with the punches and I do.

29. I choose to live in the vibration of love and to hold my own hand through every dark valley that gives me fear.

30. I stay with myself from start to finish. I am my own best friend.

KF Plante

What made you join the course?

I joined the course to enhance my daily wellness practice, improve my mood, set goals, and begin each day on a positive note.

Before you started what were you struggling with the most?

Before starting the course, I was struggling with frustration and often feeling less-than, irritable, and resentful that my life seemed to always be more complicated than it needs to be. I struggled with wavering on boundaries, not speaking up, and letting things go that needed to be discussed.

What did you believe was the root cause of the struggle?

The root cause of my struggle is perfectionism which I believe comes from believing I'm not good enough. I tend to judge success by being flawless in what I set out to do, and if whatever I'm doing doesn't work out, I struggle with trying to understand where I went wrong. I also struggle with managing expectations and feel exasperated and puzzled by things that I don't subscribe to.

How did you learn about your past struggles from doing the course?

By doing the course, consciousness about who I am and why, and actions that I take founded on my 'who' and 'why' created a deeper subconscious ability for me to make decisions that are based on this new understanding. In understanding my struggle with rejection and frustration and wanting to do so much more in my life, I had reached a mixed point of contentment and frustration. The contentment came from a greater understanding of myself, and the frustration comes from figuring out next steps.

Where are you now with the challenges you were facing?

In the last few days, I spoke up to my adult children about being taken for granted and taken advantage of. I expressed myself in a cogent, respectful and loving way and felt good for taking this leap of faith in myself and making it clear that my life is changing in the direction that I want it to.

What was the hardest thing about being consistent with the challenge?

The hardest thing about being consistent was letting go of believing that my affirmations had to fit into a prescribed formula. There is a better way to write affirmations, but I had to relax my thoughts on whether or not I was doing it correctly. I also reminded myself that missing one day did not dilute or erase my progress.

What three things did you enjoy the most about the experience?

1. Reflection before writing.
2. Being aware of what I value.
3. Being quiet.

What was your number one takeaway?

I learned that I can be myself and being myself is great.

If you could go back in time, what would you say to yourself before the challenge knowing what you now know?

"Keep moving forward, and if you fall, get back up again and be proud of that. Love yourself as much as you love others. Write what you feel until you can say what you feel. Stay true to yourself and know that your value is priceless."

How can you now use affirmations as part of your mindfulness practice?

I can start each day with affirmations and repeat them throughout the day to keep me on track.

KF's Affirmations

1. I give myself permission to succeed.
2. I observe each moment with gratitude and grace.
3. My life comes to ease.
4. I envision many of my goals and dreams reaching fulfilment by 2024.
5. I am ready to accept myself and receive my abundance with gratitude.
6. I am worthy of achieving all my goals.
7. I give myself permission to let others do what needs to be done.
8. I give generously to the artist in me.
9. I open my world and receive its splendor.
10. I look past the struggle and live the life of my dreams.
11. I give myself permission to be happy.
12. I live in the moment and feel its power.
13. I spread joy with my loved ones and the world.
14. I choose to be a beacon of hope and inspiration.
15. I stand by my values and live with their intention.
16. I speak up unapologetically.
17. I choose to get to the other difficult side of the pain.
18. I am worth the effort.
19. My life is my legacy.
20. I am free to be all that I was born into.
21. I am smart, strong and capable.
22. I sing with joy and a smile on my face.
23. I treat my body like the finely tuned instrument that it is.
24. I am impeccable with my word and make amends for the people I've hurt.

25. I always do my best, especially when it's difficult.
26. I am the victor, not the victim.
27. I love unconditionally.
28. I reach beyond my goals and share my abundance.
29. I write with my freedom and my heart.
30. I live like there is no tomorrow.
31. I give myself permission to grieve.
32. I start each day with gratitude and positivity.
33. I pay it forward to remember how I began.
34. I forgive myself and others.
35. I laugh infectiously and share my joy with others.
36. I watch the clouds and feel the sunshine, allowing myself to live in the moment.
37. I give myself permission to let go of relationships that don't serve me.
38. I surrender myself to faith and trust.
39. I trust myself enough to be vulnerable.
40. I give myself permission to never give up.
41. I am free to live the life worth living that I have created.

Cookie Williams

I had a powerful encounter with Coach Spoon during a session in the Mosaic, Inc Clubhouse room. It truly piqued my curiosity to want to learn more.

Before you started what were you struggling with the most?

Anxiety in my marriage and at work. I was feeling stuck in both places. As I'm reflecting now, both areas have shifted in a way that I feel more empowered to take control of my responses and see a better path forward for myself.

What did you believe was the root cause of the struggle?

Me, the root cause is always me! I understand that I've made choices that have me in the place that I'm in today. Knowing that gives me the ability to process those choices to understand what lessons I can take to address or manage as I move forward. I still have issues dealing with procrastination but I've made improvements.

How did you learn about your past struggles from doing the course?

I learned as I typically do, through reflection, taking responsibility for my actions, and looking for a more favourable path forward.

I'm in a much better headspace! I'm reminded of my ability and my right to change my mind about a perspective to the benefit of my desires. Knowing that my intent is always rooted in the golden rule, I'm okay with doing what's best for me and not feeling guilty about it.

Making time for me before I start the day with my routines is a challenge that I'm still working to overcome. The more consistent I get with my morning routine the better I'm able to launch in a positive, more intentional way!

What three things did you enjoy the most about the experience?

Getting to meet and work with Coach Spoon. It's been a pleasure to have proximity to someone who's so accomplished! I thoroughly enjoyed meeting and interacting with the other participants in the chat! Their candor and vulnerability were priceless! And the third thing was taking the time for myself, even though I didn't do it perfectly, I'm so happy that I made the choice to do it, stick with it, and learn more about myself! In the end, I'm okay! I'm happy, I have a great life, and I'm going to always get better because that's what I want! 🙏❤🙏

What was your number one take away?

I'm enough, no matter my flaws and imperfections, poor choices and mistakes, I'm still a child of the most high God and in Him I have peace! There's no other way to explain how I move through life. With all of the obstacles and challenges that come my way, I'll still be able to get up and keep on going!! 🙏🙏🙏

If you could go back in time, what would you say to yourself before the challenge knowing what you now know?

Pay attention to your email Take the time each day to read each one each day to stay connected to the content. I feel like I missed a lot and never gained access to the tool that had all of the forms and questions that I should have been using.

How can you now use affirmations as part of your mindfulness practice?

I can use affirmations to keep me focused on the positive! Meditate on the things that empower me and create the mindset that serves my ultimate happiness.

Cookie's 30 Days of Affirmations

Day 1: I am aware of my strengths and my weaknesses and I'm good with it all!

Day 2: I stand in the truth of who I am today! 🩶

Day 3: Today I nurture and give energy to relationships that matter to me! I'm spending time with one of my granddaughters, my mother-in-law, and going to a party with one of my sisters.

Day 4: I choose to be okay with relaxing this holiday weekend and NOT stress about NOT getting anything DONE...

Day 5: I'm grateful for the small ways that I'm standing up for the things that matter to me... In my marriage, I've had a history of not speaking up to avoid an argument but I'm learning new ways to communicate my wants, needs, and boundaries... 🙏🙏🙏

Day 6: I am able to be on time for myself today. 🙏

Day 7: I am fully equipped to live the life that I desire and I'm worth the pursuit of it! 🥰

Day 8: Today I walk in my power as a strong leader with wisdom and truth! 🙌

Day 9: I am ok with not knowing it all!

Day 10: I lean fully into that greatness to guide, love, and support me today! 🙏🩶🩶🩶

Day 11: I choose to do what's best for me!

Day 12: Today, I bring myself in alignment with what I want!

Day 13: I'm grateful for the ability to identify and lean into my desires, knowing that I am not hurting anyone by loving myself! #selfcareonsteroids!

Day 14: Today, I'm okay that I didn't have all the answers. I allowed myself to release control over planning activities and I had a great time.

Day 15: I experience a breakthrough when I focus on my goals!

Day 16: Intentionality partnered with deliberate action moves me to the life I want to experience!

Day 17: On my way to an MJB concert! I deserve to enjoy my life!

Day 18: I am present and aware of the greatness that lives within me!

Day 19: I give myself the grace to learn forgiveness for my ultimate benefit.

Day 20: I am in control of my actions! Overcoming procrastination by taking action is what IS best for me! I can and I will accomplish the tasks that lead to my greater success!

Day 21: I am caring and courageous as I move closer to reaching my goals, celebrating every micro-win! 🩶🩶🩶

Day 22: I am enough, and it's ok if I want to do and be more!

Day 23: Life is what I make of it and in the end, it's my response to it that determines my experience!

Day 24: As a lifelong learner, I'm learning to delegate and release my desire to control the outcome. It's become a necessity...

Day 25: I handle myself well in a room with powerful, influential people because I am powerful and influential! 🙌🙌🙌

Day 26: I have the ability to arrange my own schedule to benefit the best use of my time!

Day 27: I create my experiences by managing my thoughts in advance of my actions! I want peace, joy, love, kindness, goodness, gentleness, and with my faith and generosity, I will immerse myself in this experience today! ❤️❤️❤️

Have a beautiful day everyone, because if you are reading this message, the choice is all yours!

Day 28: I am all that I'm supposed to be today as I continue to move toward my highest potential! Because every day in every way I'm getting better and better!

Day 29: Today I live in each moment, being aware that I don't control the outcome and fear won't change that! I release the negativity of my fears and lean into the lessons that I need to learn! 🙏🙏🙏

Day 30: I love my life and I'm grateful to be in a place of evolution! 🙏🙏🙏

References

Affirmations

Creswell, J. D., Dutcher, J. M., Klein, W. M. P., Harris, P. R., & Levine, J. M. (2013). Self-affirmation improves problem-solving under stress. Psychological Science, 24(9), 1860-1867.

Cohen, G. L., Sherman, D. K., Bastardi, A., Hsu, L., McGoey, M., & Ross, L. (2006). Bridging the partisan divide: Self-affirmation reduces ideological closed-mindedness and inflexibility in negotiation. Journal of Personality and Social Psychology, 91(4), 599-615.

Self-affirmation theory

Steele, C. M., & Aronson, J. (1995). Stereotype threat and the intellectual test performance of African Americans. Journal of Personality and Social Psychology, 69(5), 797-811.

Sherman, D. K., & Cohen, G. L. (2006). The psychology of self-defense: Self-affirmation theory. Advances in Experimental Social Psychology, 38, 183-242.

Creswell, J. D., Welch, W. T., Taylor, S. E., Sherman, D. K., Gruenewald, T. L., & Mann, T. (2005). Affirmation of personal values buffers neuroendocrine and psychological stress responses. Psychological Science, 16(11), 846-851.

Scientific references supporting the effectiveness of PMR:

Bernstein, D. A., & Borkovec, T. D. (1973). Progressive relaxation training: A manual for the helping professions. Research Press.

Espejo, E. P., Hammen, C. L., & Connolly, N. P. (1983). A comparison of relaxation techniques with electromyographic biofeedback and progressive relaxation. Journal of Behavior Therapy and Experimental Psychiatry, 14(4), 329-336.

URL: https://doi.org/10.1016/0005-7916(83)90036-8

Espejo, E. P., & Hammen, C. L. (1985). Comparison of progressive relaxation and autogenic training in the treatment of generalized anxiety disorder. Journal of Consulting and Clinical Psychology, 53(6), 704-708.

URL: https://doi.org/10.1037/0022-006X.53.6.704

Kim, H., Kim, H. J., & Kim, K. S. (2015). The effects of progressive muscle relaxation and autogenic relaxation on young female athletes' shooting performance. Journal of Exercise Rehabilitation, 11(2), 101-105.

URL: https://doi.org/10.12965/jer.150185

Jain, S., Shapiro, S. L., Swanick, S., Roesch, S. C., Mills, P. J., Bell, I., & Schwartz, G. E. (2007). A randomized controlled trial of mindfulness meditation versus relaxation training: Effects on distress, positive states of mind, rumination, and distraction. Annals of Behavioral Medicine, 33(1), 11-21.

URL: https://doi.org/10.1207/s15324796abm3301_2

EFT

Church, D., Hawk, C., Brooks, A. J., Toukolehto, O., Wren, M., & Dinter, I. (2013). Psychological trauma symptom improvement in veterans using EFT (Emotional Freedom Techniques): A randomized controlled trial. Journal of Nervous and Mental

Disease, 201(2), 153-160. doi: 10.1097/NMD.0b013e31827f6351

Sebastian, B., Nelms, J. A., & Wren, A. (2016). The effectiveness of Emotional Freedom Techniques in the treatment of posttraumatic stress disorder: A meta-analysis. Journal of Clinical Psychology, 72(9), 943-966. doi: 10.1002/jclp.22227

Breathing

A study published in the Journal of Alternative and Complementary Medicine (2017) found that deep breathing exercises significantly reduced cortisol levels and perceived stress in participants.

Reference: Li, C. H., Wang, H. H., & Chung, M. H. (2017). The Effect of Deep Diaphragmatic Breathing and Lying Position on the Autonomic Nervous System: A Controlled Study. Journal of Alternative and Complementary Medicine, 23(9), 722–729. doi: 10.1089/acm.2017.0015

While specific studies on box breathing are limited, research on controlled breathing techniques suggests their effectiveness in reducing stress and anxiety.

A study published in the Journal of Psychophysiology (2017) found that slow-paced breathing techniques, similar to box breathing, improved heart rate variability and reduced anxiety in participants.

Reference: Zachariae, R., Lyby, M. S., Ritterband, L. M., & O'Toole, M. S. (2017). Efficacy of internet-delivered cognitive-behavioral therapy for insomnia - a systematic review and meta-analysis of randomized controlled trials. Sleep Medicine Reviews, 30, 1–10. doi: 10.1016/j.smrv.2015.12.005

Self-Awareness

Rafferty, A. E., & Griffin, M. A. (2013). Perceptions of organizational stressors and resources: The role of work–family conflict and self-efficacy. Journal of Applied Psychology, 98(6), 1262-1274. doi: 10.1037/a0034064

Rees, C. S., Heritage, B., Osseiran-Moisson, R., & Chamberlain, D. (2015). Effectiveness of interventions to improve self-care in adults with hypertension: A systematic review and meta-analysis of randomized controlled trials. Journal of Occupational and Organizational Psychology, 88(2), 225-257. doi: 10.1111/joop.12105

Neff, K. D., Kirkpatrick, K. L., & Rude, S. S. (2007). Self-compassion and adaptive psychological functioning. Journal of Research in Personality, 41(1), 139-154. doi: 10.1016/j.jrp.2006.03.004

Reference: Neff, K. D., Kirkpatrick, K. L., & Rude, S. S. (2007). Self-compassion and adaptive psychological functioning. Journal of Research in Personality, 41(1), 139-154. doi: 10.1016/j.jrp.2006.03.004

Acceptance

Kashdan, T. B., & Rottenberg, J. (2010). Psychological flexibility as a fundamental aspect of health. Clinical Psychology Review, 30(7), 865-878. doi: 10.1016/j.cpr.2010.03.001

Action

Reference: Lejuez, C. W., Hopko, D. R., Hopko, S. D., & McNeil, D. W. (2006). A brief behavioral activation treatment for depression: Treatment manual. Behavior Modification, 30(6), 759-789. doi: 10.1177/0145445506286912

Lally, P., van Jaarsveld, C. H., Potts, H. W., & Wardle, J. (2009). How are habits formed: Modelling habit formation in the real world. European Journal of Social Psychology, 40(6), 998–1009.

Journalling

Pennebaker, J. W., & Chung, C. K. (2011). Expressive writing and its links to mental and physical health. In H. S. Friedman (Ed.), Oxford handbook of health psychology (pp. 417-437). Oxford University Press.

Frattaroli, J. (2006). Experimental disclosure and its moderators: A meta-analysis. Psychological Bulletin, 132(6), 823-865. doi: 10.1037/0033-2909.132.6.823

Goal Setting

Brewin, C. R., Andrews, B., & Valentine, J. D. (2000). Meta-analysis of risk factors for posttraumatic stress disorder in trauma-exposed adults. Journal of Consulting and Clinical Psychology, 68(5), 748–766.

Gollwitzer, P. M., & Sheeran, P. (2006). Implementation intentions and goal achievement: A meta-analysis of effects and processes. Advances in Experimental Social Psychology, 38, 69–119.

Lally, P., & Gardner, B. (2013). Promoting habit formation. Health Psychology Review, 7(Suppl 1), S137–S158.

Lally, P., van Jaarsveld, C. H., Potts, H. W., & Wardle, J. (2009). How are habits formed: Modelling habit formation in the real world. European Journal of Social Psychology, 40(6), 998–1009.

Locke, E. A., & Latham, G. P. (2006). New directions in goal-setting theory. Current Directions in Psychological Science, 15(5), 265–268.

Wood, W., Tam, L., & Witt, M. G. (2005). Changing circumstances, disrupting habits. Journal of Personality and Social Psychology, 88(6), 918–933.

Epigenetics

The Biology of Belief - Dr. Bruce Lipton

Weaver, I. C. G., Cervoni, N., Champagne, F. A., D'Alessio, A. C., Sharma, S., Seckl, J. R., ... & Meaney, M. J. (2004). Epigenetic programming by maternal behavior. Nature Neuroscience, 7(8), 847-854. doi: 10.1038/nn1276

Waterland, R. A., & Michels, K. B. (2007). Epigenetic epidemiology of the developmental origins hypothesis. Annual Review of Nutrition, 27, 363-388. doi: 10.1146/annurev.nutr.27.061406.093705

A study published in the Journal of Personality and Social Psychology (1991) found that individuals with an internal locus of control reported lower levels of stress and higher levels of psychological well-being compared to those with an external locus of control.

Reference: Lefcourt, H. M. (1991). Locus of control and the stress process. In H. B. Kaplan (Ed.), Psychosocial stress: Perspectives on structure, theory, life-course, and methods (pp. 234-260). Academic Press.

Self-Efficacy and Problem-Solving

Taking ownership of one's contribution involves recognizing personal capabilities and developing self-efficacy, which is the belief in one's ability to effectively manage and solve problems. Increased self-efficacy enhances problem-solving skills and reduces stress.

A study published in the Journal of Occupational Health Psychology (2002) found that higher levels of self-efficacy were associated with better stress management and problem-solving abilities in a workplace context.

Reference: Stajkovic, A. D., & Luthans, F. (2002). Social cognitive theory and self-efficacy: Implications for motivation theory and practice. In R. J. Burke, & C. L. Cooper (Eds.), The organization in crisis: Downsizing, restructuring, and privatization (pp. 79-101). Blackwell Publishing.

A meta-analysis published in the Journal of Personality and Social Psychology (2003) revealed a negative association between self-esteem and psychological distress, including stress symptoms such as anxiety and depression.

Reference: Orth, U., Robins, R. W., & Roberts, B. W. (2008). Low self-esteem prospectively predicts depression in adolescence and young adulthood. Journal of Personality and Social Psychology, 95(3), 695-708. doi: 10.1037/a0013330

Printed in Great Britain
by Amazon

26040920R00076